WHAT SHAKESPEARE TEACHES US ABOUT PSYCHOANALYSIS

WHAT SHAKESPEARE TEACHES US ABOUT PSYCHOANALYSIS
A Local Habitation and a Name

*Dorothy T. Grunes and
Jerome M. Grunes*

KARNAC

First published in 2014 by
Karnac Books Ltd
118 Finchley Road
London NW3 5HT

Copyright © 2014 by Dorothy T. Grunes and Jerome M. Grunes

The rights of Dorothy T. Grunes and Jerome M. Grunes to be identified as the authors of this work has been asserted in accordance with §§ 77 and 78 of the Copyright Design and Patents Act 1988.

All rights reserved. No part of this publication may be reproduced, stored in a retrieval system, or transmitted, in any form or by any means, electronic, mechanical, photocopying, recording, or otherwise, without the prior written permission of the publisher.

British Library Cataloguing in Publication Data

A C.I.P. for this book is available from the British Library

ISBN-13: 978-1-78220-136-6

Typeset by V Publishing Solutions Pvt Ltd., Chennai, India

Printed in Great Britain

www.karnacbooks.com

I would not wish
Any companion in the world but you.

(*The Tempest*, III.i.60–61)

We would like to dedicate this book to our dear friends, colleagues, teachers and students at The Chicago Institute for Psychoanalysis, The American Psychoanalytic Association, The American College of Psychoanalysis, The International Psychoanalytic Association, The Royal Shakespeare Company, Karnac Books, and to our absent friends who left us too soon.

I would like to thank my mother, and my siblings—Allen, Reba, Tina, and Louis, for their unconditional support. (D. T. G.)

CONTENTS

ABOUT THE AUTHORS ix

PREFACE xi

INTRODUCTION
On drama and psychoanalysis xiii

CHAPTER ONE
The metaphysics and metapsychology of evil in *Othello* 1

CHAPTER TWO
Mothers in Shakespeare—absent and present 17

CHAPTER THREE
Disguise and disavowal in *The Merchant of Venice* and
   Romeo and Juliet 51

CHAPTER FOUR
Visions of self in *Julius Caesar* 83

CHAPTER FIVE
Madness and the death of self in *Titus Andronicus*   115

CHAPTER SIX
The future of an illusionist   137

CHAPTER SEVEN
What Shakespeare teaches us about aging parents and their adult children in *King Lear*   161

AFTERWORD   181

REFERENCES   183

INDEX   187

PREFACE

Our title "A Local Habitation and a Name", suggests a specific function of literary theory. Like "the poet's pen", the role of theory is to locate and describe what we feel but do not have the language to know:

> ... and gives to airy nothing
> A local habitation and a name. (*A Midsummer Night's Dream*, V.i.17–18)

This book began as a series of lectures we gave at The Chicago Psychoanalytic Society, The American Psychoanalytic Association and The International Psychoanalytic Association. Our intended audiences are students of literature, literary theory, dramatic arts, psychoanalytic theory, and psychology, but hope it is also appealing to readers, theatregoers and those who have an interest in the human condition.

Literary criticism of William Shakespeare's work began during his lifetime and has continued to the present day. Of course, even Ben Jonson responded to the rumour that Shakespeare never edited out a line "... would he had blotted out a thousand" (Jonson, 1641, p. 52).

Psychoanalytic literary theory, historically, has either been written by psychologists who knew little about literary criticism or by literary theorists who knew little about psychoanalysis. It is not surprising that this potentially enriching combination of literary theory and psychoanalysis has had difficulty sustaining its relevance and tends towards reductionism.

Our goal is to use William Shakespeare's work as a starting point to expand our understanding of drama. Ideally, psychoanalysts should be truth seekers, who are not content until approaching that goal. In looking at literature we are at a disadvantage, as psychoanalysts do not otherwise have a value system built in of good *vs.* bad, an ability, for better or worse, that belongs solely to the realm of literary theory proper. Literary theories, in turn, often find in Shakespeare what the investigator already has concluded. The urgency of this book lies in the danger of those theories, as they seem to tell us as a society what art we keep and what art we discard. As we are both scholars of literature and psychoanalysis we are able to write with what is available in both canons. One finds the cathartic experience of drama stirs within each of us an individual experience, due to our unique make-up and life events—to feel those affects, of which even we ourselves may be unaware. Great art expresses something of humanity in such a way that even the artist himself does not "know" in a conscious way all that he reveals. In an attempt to avoid speculation of the author's inner workings, we will only respond to what the text suggests and can teach us with our even hovering attention. If we succeed in simply encouraging readers to take part in the drama and in the analytic process, rather than to be passively entertained, we will have succeeded.

D.T.G and J.M.G
Chicago, Illinois

INTRODUCTION

On drama and psychoanalysis

Psychoanalysis has from its very beginning been informed by theatre and the language of the stage. We think in terms of acting, acting out, enacting. Even the concept of the self—the true self and the false self—derives from the lexicon of actors. The metaphorical language of psychoanalysis appears when we speak of setting the stage. Perhaps there is no aspect as poignant as the role of the analyst, where we act as the chorus for the patient, and perhaps as actor too. This can be a one-person drama, a two-person drama, or a three-person drama. We can see why Sigmund Freud was so enamoured with William Shakespeare and with theatre.

In Shakespeare's dramas, characters develop—rather than simply unfold—as a result of reconceiving themselves. How this reconception takes place is of great significance, since it is close to our own clinical work. Harold Bloom attributes this process to the characters "overhearing" themselves (Bloom, 1998, pp. xix–xxii). This transcends all theories, if for no other reason than the centrality of the analyst/audience in psychoanalysis. Are we not as psychoanalysts the hearers of unconscious thoughts, feelings and fantasies? And do we not attempt to have our patients hear themselves through us? For Bloom this "self-hearing" is the royal road to individuation, as the dream was to Freud. In fact, we are much like the dramatist or at least the stage director. We set this stage using the couch and create a relatively quiet backdrop. The context of the drama is the patient's personal narrative. We move from a one-actor to a two-person drama. We are assigned parts in the transferences that we have not written. When we transgress in these experiences, and our countertransferences lead us to write our own lines, then there is the need to edit out our monologues and return to the author's (patient's) script. If we are successful the creative process of psychoanalysis takes place for both the patient and the analyst.

The shift from the office to D. W. Winnicott's potential space (Winnicott, 1971, pp. 40–41) allows the analyst to create something that has not yet been. What had previously been repressed or disavowed can come to centre stage. Instead of an actor reading lines, the patient becomes, in some way, more real to themselves as the process of analysis continues. Was it drama or analysis that was described as a "suspension of disbelief"? The patient knows we are not father, mother, or any aspect of the self, yet during the analytic hours we seem all of those and much more. When Winnicott describes the "spontaneous gesture" (Winnicott, 1965, pp. 140–152) it is the revision of a previous script. Much like Shakespeare's creation of characters, patients develop the ability to create who they really are. Freud, as early as *The Interpretation of Dreams*, parallels the stories of Oedipus and Hamlet. He writes:

> Another of the great creations of tragic poetry, Shakespeare's Hamlet, has its roots in the same soil as Oedipus Rex. But the changed treatment of the same material reveals the whole difference in the mental life of these two widely separated epochs of civilization: the secular advance of repression in the emotional life of mankind. In the Oedipus the child's wishful phantasy that underlies it is brought into the open and realized as it would be in a dream. In Hamlet it remains repressed; and just as in the case of a neurosis,—we only learn of its existence from its inhibiting consequences. (Freud, 1900a, p. 264)

Freud then suggests that the motive for Hamlet's hesitation to avenge his father (the task assigned him by the ghost) has not to do with action paralysed by intellect, as Goethe and others propose. Freud points out that Hamlet acted aggressively twice; once in the impulsive killing of

Polonius, and then as a Machiavellian prince, when he craftily sent Rosencrantz and Guildenstern to their deaths. He sees in Hamlet's distaste for sexuality in the scenes with Ophelia very much the repressed wishes that motivate his guilt and self-loathing. He further notes that Shakespeare's father died in 1601 when the play was written and supposes that the ambivalence towards the father was freshly revived. He finds parallels between Hamlet and Shakespeare's dead son Hamnet. Freud writes "… all genuinely creative writings are the product of more than a single motive and more than a single impulse in the poet's mind, and are open to more than a single interpretation" (Freud, 1900a, p. 266). Later, Freud takes up Hamlet, but this time from the perspective of the audience. Freud writes: "Here the struggle that causes the suffering is fought out in the hero's mind itself—a struggle between different impulses, and one which must have its end in the extinction, not of the hero, but of one of his impulses; it must end, that is to say, in a renunciation" (Freud, 1942a, p. 308). For the Greeks, the precondition of drama is the human struggle against the divine. Tragedy, then, is a case of rebellion against the gods in which the dramatist and the audience take the side of the rebel. When there is a loss of belief, human affairs demand central focus and Freud defined these struggles against society as "social tragedies" (Freud, 1942a, p. 264). A sub-class is the struggle between individual heroes who have freed themselves from the bonds of human institutions which Freud termed "the drama of character". Drama of character represents another shift in the central conflict, here the conflict is between two conscious impulses, and the source of the suffering is between a conscious impulse and a repressed one.

> Here the precondition of enjoyment is that the spectator should himself be a neurotic, for it is only such people who can derive pleasure instead of simple aversion from the revelation and the more or less conscious recognition of a repressed impulse. In anyone who is not neurotic this recognition will meet only with aversion and will call up a readiness to repeat the act of repression which has earlier been successfully brought to bear on the impulse: for in such people a single expenditure of repression has been enough to hold the repressed impulse completely in check. But in neurotics the repression is on the brink of failing; it is unstable and needs a constant renewal of expenditure, and this expenditure is spared if recognition of the impulse is brought about. Thus it is only in

neurotics that a struggle can occur of a kind which can be made the subject of a drama; but even in them the dramatist will provoke not merely an enjoyment of the liberation but a resistance to it as well. (Freud, 1942a, p. 309)

The three conditions that Freud indicated as necessary for the psychopathological drama are: (1) The hero becomes psychopathic in the course of the play (2) The repressed impulse is universal and (3) "… that the impulse that is struggled with is never given a definitive name; so that in the spectator too the process is carried through with his attention averted, and he is in the grip of his emotions instead of taking stock of what is happening" (Freud, 1942a, p. 309). Here Freud recognises the similarity between psychoanalysis and drama, saying "a certain amount of resistance is, no doubt, saved in this way, just as in analytic treatment, we find derivatives of the repressed material reaching consciousness, owing to a lower resistance, while the repressed material itself is unable to do so" (Freud, 1942a, p. 309). Freud then takes an unusual bow by suggesting that the true meaning of the conflict between the conscious impulse and the unconscious one he alone has been able to decipher. In conclusion we find it ironic that in *Hamlet* it is Polonius who advocates self-understanding and the play's wisest words thus fall from the mouth of a fool:

> This above all: to thine own self be true,
> And it must follow as the night the day
> Thou canst not then be false to any man. (I.iii.78–80)

CHAPTER ONE

The metaphysics and metapsychology of evil in *Othello*

From the simplistic duality of the Middle Ages, William Shakespeare was the first, in the English language, to craft characters with an understanding of the unconscious and the inner conflicts that motivate our species. It is no wonder that Sigmund Freud was so enamoured of Shakespeare that he learned English specifically to read Shakespeare's writings in its original language.

Shakespeare went beyond the stock characters of the morality plays that preceded him, with their overt personifications of virtue and vice, and gave us, for the first time, human "villains". These were different from the allegorical villains that had been in repertoire. Here we find each one has his or her own history, which, brought to the drama, does much to further our understanding of their motivations. For instance, Richard III concisely describes his version of his early life. He says that he was not fully formed before being expelled from the womb. Born prematurely he is:

> Cheated of feature by dissembling nature
> Deform'd, unfinish'd, sent before my time
> Into this breathing world, scarce half made up

> And that so lamely and unfashionable
> That dogs bark at me, as I halt by them. (I.i.19–23)

Richard believes that his early physical life has misshaped his body and has caused a resultant misshapening of his internal world. While Shakespeare expands on the character's motivations, at the very least, Richard's version of these events gives him a concretised metaphor, a screen memory (Freud, 1899a, pp. 301–322) that functions as his own personal creation myth. Richard has cleanly intellectualised his misshapen character and may now easily rationalise his misshapen actions.

Aaron the Moor, a minor figure in a difficult play, is less developed. Aaron, a warring man, lost his battle to Titus Andronicus. Unlike Richard III , we know little more about him other than he is a soldier, an African, and an outsider. Despite his villainy, the loss he suffers is profound. As he is led off to his death he says one of the most haunting lines in all of Shakespeare:

> If one good deed in all my life I did,
> I do repent it from my very soul. (V.iii.190–191)

In his final moment he says he regrets all human kindness he may have performed. However, even though the world feels meaningless his behaviour illustrates this is not so. He is redeemed, for he protects his child. While Aaron repents any kindness with his words, his son remains an exception.

In *King Lear* the villainy of many characters is complex and reminds us that there are conscious and unconscious motivations (Freud, 1915e, pp. 161–215) within each role in the play. Those whose motivations are beyond their awareness leave us to feel the burden of their ambivalence. Cordelia denies her father's veiled request to soothe him, and Edgar walks his beloved father Gloucester through a mock suicide before reuniting with him. Shakespeare has deported their own aggression and destruction from their awareness and leaves us to struggle through these characters' internal conflicts. Edmund, Gloucester's bastard son, along with Goneril and Regan are our manifest villains. It seems we refer to them as such not because they are the most cruel, but rather because they illustrate no such internal struggle. Yet we have some sympathy for Edmund as we are impressed by his cunning and machinations. With this sympathy we more easily identify with his struggle when Edmund says:

> Well, my legitimate, if this letter speed
> And my invention thrive, Edmund the base
> Shall top the legitimate. I grow, I prosper
> Now gods, stand up for bastards! (I.ii.19–22)

While one doesn't "like" Edmund, we initially feel his lot is unfair. We are drawn into his plan to frame his brother and are at least impressed by his ability to accurately identify and play on his brother's disavowed weaknesses.

These "villains", however, are very different from Iago in *Othello*.

For the majority of his plays, Shakespeare incorporated many different sources. In writing *Othello* he did something different. He based his *Othello* very closely on only one text, the play *Hecatommithi* written by Giraldi Cinthio in 1565. What we also find interesting is how Shakespeare chose to use this source. The source describes Iago's love for Desdemona.

> The wicked Ensign, taking no account of the faith he had pledged to his wife, and of the friendship, loyalty and obligations he owed the Moor, fell ardently in love with Disdemona … (Cinthio, reprinted in Honigmann, 1997, p. 373)

Shakespeare removed this. Had Iago loved Desdemona, Iago would have been similar to Richard III, Edmund, or even Aaron the Moor. Iago's motivations would be understandable. By removing this piece of the plot Shakespeare's Iago now represents a very different villain from his contemporaries and from that of Giraldi Cinthio, and even from villains of his own creation. For if, like its source, Iago is in love with Desdemona, certainly we would understand that he is motivated by competition with Othello. When Shakespeare removed the love plot he removed sustainable motivation for Iago's actions. Samuel Taylor Coleridge described this as Iago's "motiveless malignity" (Coleridge, 1849, p. 262). We will attempt to discover what drives Iago through the use of psychoanalytic concepts and close textual analysis.

As the play opens, Iago expresses his hatred of Othello for having ranked Michael Cassio above him. Iago says: "I know my price, I am worth no worse a place" (I.i.10). Perhaps Iago is attempting to soothe himself by using memory of his previous successes to restore the self that has just been injured (Kohut, 1984, pp. 49–63). It seems that in simply reminding himself of his own "price" his apparent need to restore the self dissipates. Iago says: "In following him I follow but myself" (I.i.57). The narcissistic blow that we are led to think is the motivation for Iago has been removed by the poet's pen just as suddenly as it was added. It does not further organise Iago. We would posit that the narcissistic slight is superficial and does not cut into Iago's view of himself. Iago states:

> But I will wear my heart upon my sleeve
> For daws to peck at: I am not what I am. (I.i.63–64)

This last phrase reverses God's reply to Moses when he said: "I am what I am", thus throwing the audience into the metaphysical mode. Shakespeare uncharacteristically references the Bible. The play here reverts to a morality play of the Middle Ages.

While Othello and Desdemona elope in the night, Iago orders Roderigo to wake Desdemona's father Brabantio. Iago introduces the metaphors of poison and magic, saying: "Rouse him, make after him, poison his delight ..." (I.i.67). These images persist throughout the drama as a concretisation of a primitive sense of causality. When Brabantio meets with the Duke, and the Venetian senators, he says that Othello has: "... Abused her delicate youth with drugs or minerals ..." (I.ii.74). Poisons are unknown, sensed but not experienced but by their outcome. They are a magic in that they are actively incorporated but passively experienced. It represents the shift from secondary to primary process thinking (Freud, 1950a, pp. 295–387). Thus, as the play regresses from secondary to primary process by reverting from Elizabethan drama to the morality plays of the church, so too do the characters here revert to primary process by changing morality from active to magical. The morality changes from what one strives for to what one has without effort.

Othello clearly idealises Venice, and Desdemona its pearl. Othello tries to identify with its court by over-reaching them. Although the Venetians, blaming magic for Desdemona's love, threaten Othello with prison—Othello's idealisation of the court remains unchanged, or if not it becomes a more desperate one. Othello's language here reflects an even more strenuous attempt to identify with the Venetians. His language becomes precious, careful, rehearsed, and his resulting speeches are almost unintelligible as he replies with excessive syllables, such as: "May speak unbonneted" (I.ii.23), and "unhoused free condition" (I.ii.26). This stilted language contrasts to Iago's almost melodically constructed speech. As an outsider he not only attempts to assimilate, but he must be more Venetian than the Venetians.

These two characters, Othello and Iago, have a drive for their narrative to be told and to be responded to. Othello tells Desdemona of his past, enticing her, and with her affect the telling re-establishes a sense of self for Othello. Othello's adventures enchant Desdemona. Othello relates Desdemona's response:

> ... if I had a friend that loved her,
> I should but teach him how to tell my story
> And that would woo her. (I.iii.165–167)

He tells her of:

> ... cannibals that each other eat,
> The Anthropophagi, and men whose heads
> Do grow beneath their shoulders. (I.iii.144–146)

Othello is not simply describing his adventures of his past; he is also introducing us to the oral aggressive and the consuming nature of Venice in the present. Iago's wife, Emilia, takes up this theme, as she says:

> 'Tis not a year or two shows us a man.
> They are all but stomachs, and we all but food:
> To eat us hungerly, and when they are full
> They belch us ... (III.iv.103–106)

Cannibalism is not only oral sadism but is an identification—that is, to orally ingest characteristics of the other. Othello took in and internalised Venice, and will be consumed by Venice in turn. Othello says that Desdemona would: "... with a greedy ear devour up my discourse ..." (I.iii.149–150). The theme of the stories he tells is of his escapes. "Greedy" Desdemona takes in his narrative and identifies with it. It touches great depths and allows her to: "… fall in love with what she fear'd to look on." (I.iii.99). Telling his adventures revives him, as does Desdemona's response to the tales, yet this may leave him profoundly vulnerable.

> She loved me for the dangers I had pass'd
> And I loved her that she did pity them. (I.iii.168–169)

He escapes slavery and cannibalism but will not be able to survive Desdemona's love.

The Turkish fleet is invading Venetian lands alleging that they are headed for Rhodes. This ploy is like Iago's subterfuge. While the senators recognise the Turkish decoy:

> … 'tis a pageant
> To keep us in false gaze. (I.iii.19–20)

It emphasises Iago's deceptions and underscores every character's inability to perceive them.

Roderigo loves Desdemona. Iago is disgusted by affect:

> … I never found a man
> that knew how to love himself. Ere I would say, I
> would drown myself for the love of a guinea-hen, I
> would change my humanity with a baboon. (I.iii.313–316)

It is not simply that Iago cannot tolerate affect. His definition of what it is to be human is to be one without emotions. Like Othello, Iago also has a need to tell his story. Instead of Desdemona it is us who are Iago's audience. Thus Iago begins his frequent monologues, soliloquies, and asides. As he speaks directly to us, he ingratiates, seduces, and makes us his co-conspirators. Because Iago chooses to interact with the audience, an imagined other, rather than another character on the stage, we further understand that he does not value human interaction. Iago sees without passion, which distorts the vision of others. He is illusion-less. He sees the self-deception that other people live by and uses this knowledge to undo them. Iago lushly describes this phenomenon:

> Virtue! a fig!'Tis in ourselves that we are thus, or
> thus. Our bodies are gardens, to the which our

> wills are gardeners. So that if we will plant nettles
> or sow lettuce, set hyssop and weed up thyme, supply
> it with one gender of herbs or distract it with many,
> either to have it sterile with idleness or manured with
> industry—why, the power and corrigible authority of
> this lies in our wills. If the balance of our lives had not
> one scale of reason to poise another of sensuality, the
> blood and baseness of our natures would conduct us
> to most preposterous conclusions. But we have
> reason to cool our raging motions, our carnal
> strings, our unbitted lusts; whereof I take this, that
> you call love, to be a sect or scion. (I.iii.320–333)

Love is not part of human nature but rather is grafted on. He tells us that we all have false selves (Winnicott, 1960, pp. 140–152). In his garden are aerophytes without roots. His plottings can be quickly reorganised and mobilised. None are deeply cathected. His language suggests a fullness but is, instead, empty. This is the barren Garden of Eden.

Love, he explains:

> … is merely a lust of the blood and a permission of
> the will. Come, be a man. Drown thyself! drown
> cats and blind puppies. (I.iii.335–337)

Iago views all affect as invasive and illusory. Human interaction is that which takes something away from you or your view of what you yourself should be. Portia and Juliet, although they come to different ends, both give all, and put themselves in danger for the sake of love. To Iago, affect is automatically self-destructive. When one loses any aspect of oneself it is destructive. This reveals the egocentricity of Iago. He encourages Roderigo to project affect onto animals, which will not fight back. Any contact with another will destroy you. In the case of Othello, Iago is correct.

Iago speaks to the audience:

> … I hate the
> Moor and it is thought abroad that 'twixt my sheets
> He has done my office. I know not if't be true
> But I for mere suspicion in that kind
> Will do as if for surety. (I.iii.385–389)

This rumour that Othello had sex with Iago's wife Emilia serves as the germ of an idea to advance his plot. For Iago, true or false, it has no substance. However, Iago is able to discern those who are susceptible. Iago recognises if he himself is susceptible this could only weaken him, therefore Iago stores rumoured adultery away in his arsenal to later undo Othello. For Othello, unlike Iago, affect is authentic, and infidelity and loss is feared and is of catastrophic proportions.

> ... He holds me well,
> The better shall my purpose work on him.
> Cassio's a proper man: let me see now,
> To get his place, and to plume up my will
> In double knavery. How? How? Let's see ... (I.iii.389–393)

Here we see Iago's mind at work. Iago creates his own play unbeknownst to the actors of it. This is not the actual play within the play of *Hamlet* or *A Midsummer Night's Dream*. Iago casts Othello as jealous, Cassio as romantic, and Desdemona as untrue. They embrace these roles and believe them to be themselves. Thus Iago turns actor into character. They no longer act, but become. Perhaps Iago, like the great illusionist Prospero, is a rendition of Shakespeare himself, and suggests something more sinister about the creative process.

> After some time to abuse Othello's ear
> That he is too familiar with his wife
> He hath a person and a smooth dispose
> To be suspected, framed to make women false.
> The Moor is of a free and open nature
> That think men honest that but seem to be so ... (I.iii.394–399)

He continues:

> ... I have't it. It is engendered! Hell and night
> Must bring this monstrous birth to the world's light.
> (I.iii.402–403)

The experience of watching a play is a complicated one. Not only is the audience privy to the thoughts and plotting of Iago, but we become part of it. The audience is necessary to create and maintain Iago. Here we are the transitional object (Winnicott, 1958, pp. 229–242) that Iago requires to ease him and his nefarious plans, and we are helpless to do anything to interfere with them. We are part of the engendering and the midwife for the birth of the drama.

We begin in Venice, and as the scene shifts the great Venetian explorers bring us to Cyprus , far from the centre of power. Through references and metaphor we travel from Aleppo to North Africa, from Egypt to Cyprus, and from Jerusalem to Spain. We move to the very edge of civilisation. These exotic, faraway places, wherever we travel, will lead us all to our true selves. Unlike *The Tempest*, *As You Like It*, or *King Lear*, this voyage into nature changes more in the audience and less in the characters. The danger in the play, as if somehow resilient to change, now casts a shadow across the entire globe.

A great tempest is raging. Desdemona is anxiously awaiting news of Othello's fate at sea. Strangely, at this frightening moment she uses Iago to calm and ease her anxieties, as one would use a court jester; if not to actually allay discomforts, at least to distract from them. While Iago tells his crass puns and derides the virtues of women, simultaneously his mind is active and he is contriving how he will use Cassio and Desdemona for his purposes. He addresses the audience:

> … as little a web as this will I
> ensnare as great a fly as Cassio. Ay, smile upon
> her, do: I will gyve thee in thine own courtship. (II.i.161–163)

Iago suspects that Cassio may indeed love Desdemona and will use this to his advantage. He continues: "The Moor! I know his trumpet!" (II.i.178). Iago refers to both the trumpet that heralds Othello's return and to Othello's vulnerability. He also believes Desdemona would cuckold Othello. He reveals this to Roderigo:

> Mark me with what violence she first loved the Moor,
> but for bragging and telling fantastical lies:
> and will she love him still for prating? (II.i.220–222)

Unlike Othello, Iago is unmoved by the telling of his tale. Neither revenge nor success seems to gratify or organise him. Iago creates the illusion of an affair and returns briefly to a revenge motif. However, he knows that passion is poison to him.

When Cassio will not seduce Desdemona, Iago immediately homes in on Cassio's awareness that he is not masculine. As Iago sings: "Why then let a soldier drink!" (II.iii.69). He is underlining that Cassio is not a soldier, and questions if he is a real man. Touching Cassio's vulnerability, Cassio takes up the challenge, becoming uncharacteristically drunk and riotous. Othello, furious for being interrupted in his wedding bed, demotes Cassio and names Iago his second in command. This promotion is the promotion Iago has been seeking since the play's beginning. We wanted to see this as repair for Iago's narcissistic slight, but the promotion has no meaning to him. Iago admits to us if he were indeed cuckolded by Othello it is of no consequence. Cassio is humiliated and seeks comfort from Iago. Iago soothes him:

> Reputation is an idle and most false
> imposition: oft got without merit and lost without
> deserving. (II.iii.264–266)

Although Iago has Cassio demoted in front of his own eyes. It seems that the characters look to Iago in a distorted way because they want to be deceived. Iago tells each what they want to hear, or need to hear, to follow Iago's machinations. These lines on reputation differ from his words to Othello in the following act when Iago says:

> 'Twas mine,'tis his, and has been slaves to thousands—
> But he that filches from me my good name
> Robs me of that which not enriches him
> And makes me poor indeed! (III.iii.161–164)

This group of strikingly discordant characters all seem to become more dissimilar to each other the further they travel from Venice. The one trait that is magnified on their voyage is that each character finds Iago to be true. The only two to question these virtues are Emilia and Roderigo and even they underestimate Iago's malevolence. As late as the Act IV, Roderigo notices that: "… your words and performances are no kin together" (IV.ii.184–185).

Iago's own plotting is reminiscent of the poisoning of Hamlet's father:

> I'll pour this pestilence into his ear:
> That she repeals him for her body's lust.

> And by how much she strives to do him good
> She shall undo her credit with the Moor—
> So will I turn her virtue into pitch
> And out of her own goodness make the net
> That shall enmesh them all. (II.iii.351–357)

We too get entangled in his web and are accepting of his conspiracy. As the play has taken Othello out of Venice and left him without the protection of the actual physical idealised city he now must rely on his internal version of his introject (Freud, 1917e, pp. 243–258). As Iago manipulates Othello's jealousy and suspicion of Desdemona he is seemingly cautioning Othello with a metaphor of magic and orality:

> O beware, my lord, of jealousy!
> It is the green-eyed monster, which doth mock
> The meat it feeds on … (III.iii.167–169)

Othello becomes certain of Desdemona's infidelity, and we become aware of how much he needs her and the Venice she personifies.

> Her name, that was as fresh
> As Dian's visage, is now begrimed and black
> As mine own face. (III.iii.389–391)

When Othello's passions arise he senses that at his core he is a great destructive machine saved only by his idealising love of Desdemona. He muses:

> But I do love thee! And when I love thee not
> Chaos is come again. (III.iii.91–92)

He has known chaos before. For the first time, Othello's language is loosened. His speech is no longer an impersonation of the court and he rages: "I'll tear her all to pieces!" (III.iii.434). Unlike the journeys of Hamlet, Lear, or even Macbeth, the change in Othello occurs very rapidly. Iago gloats hypnotically:

> Not poppy nor mandragora
> Nor all the drowsy syrups of the world
> Shall ever medicine thee to that sweet sleep
> Which thou owedst yesterday. (III.iii.333–336)

Similar to the weird sisters in *Macbeth*, the primitive elements of the play break through from the earth into the court with references to the elements of sulfur, chrysolite, poppy, and mandrake. So too do the primitive drives become apparent beneath the court's facade.

Iago understands that Othello needs little evidence to prove Desdemona's unfaithfulness; however, he asks Emilia to steal the handkerchief anyway. Only after the handkerchief is gone does Othello reveal its meaning to Desdemona:

> 'Tis true, there's magic in the web of it.
> A sibyl that had number'd in the world
> The sun to course two hundred compasses
> In her prophetic fury sew'd the work;
> The worms were hallow'd that did breed the silk,
> And it was dyed in mummy, which the skilful
> Conserv'd of maidens' hearts. (III.iv.71–77)

This handkerchief was woven of embalmed body parts, not unlike primitive part objects (Klein, Heinmann, Issacs, & Riviere, 1952, pp. 122–168). When pressed by her husband to produce the handkerchief, Desdemona lies and says it is not lost. Iago's stagecraft is now working on Desdemona, and she plays the part Iago has cast her in. The handkerchief is a token of a soothing aspect of his past and a transitional object for Othello. Seeing Bianca with the handkerchief is Othello's final undoing. His idealisation of Venice, power, and purity, as symbolised by Desdemona, becomes baseless and the loss of the idealisation is the loss of his projected self. Othello plans to poison her. Iago dissuades him: "Do it not with poison, strangle her in her bed" (IV.i.204). Poison is passive and symbolic. Iago manipulates and reveals what is unknown within each character. He opens for the inhibited all that has previously been forbidden and watches them destroy themselves with this. Iago needs Othello to be active. Only then will Othello's defences break apart and he will no longer be able to rationalise his aggressive impulses, as his true self will break free.

Othello suffocates Desdemona in their bed. Emilia is killed as the villainy of Iago is exposed. This does not stop him. Evil, unlike revenge, cannot be part of symptom formation. It does not contain Iago.

Iago does not assuage Othello's guilt for murdering his wife, nor for murdering his own wife, nor does he glory in the recognition of his villainy, but rather Iago says to Othello with his very last line: "… What you know, you know" (V.ii.300). Iago is not killed and thus evil does not end. The play cannot conclude, even when the curtain falls.

We attempted to understand Iago as a character suffering from a narcissistic slight, overwhelmed by rage, but the text would not support it. We thought of him as a jealous husband, traumatised by his wife's infidelity, thus thrusting his own feelings into Othello's consciousness, yet this is contrary to his affectless state.

Beyond good and bad, we have focused on the evil in Iago. He is the true protagonist. His monologues are many times that of Othello's and he is on stage for most of the play. As much as he is an anti-hero, he fascinates us with his intelligence, his elevated language, and the glee he has in managing his many plots. He maintains his heroic quality even after he is exposed by Othello. He will not defend himself. The statement, "I am what I am" clearly is self-deceptive. If he and we had more time, his deeds would continue, for he shows no regrets on playing on the jealousy of Othello and the virtue of Desdemona. He is not a fallen angel like Satan nor will he ever suffer the pains of hell. He is an artist. Johann Wolfgang von Goethe's Faust merely wants to be young and virile and to be freed from an intellectual harness. That Margaret was a virtuous and saintly virgin was not his concern. He could have just as easily debauched with someone else. Iago sees virtue and attacks it because it exists. He plays on the ambivalence of his victims and turns their supposed strength into character flaws.

He is the only one in the play that has no lineage. The Moor came from Africa, Desdemona from Venice, Cassio from Florence, but where did Iago spring from? At the onset, it seems that his jealousy of Cassio has started him on a journey for revenge but this is dispelled when Othello himself comes into view. Iago quickly recognises the self-doubt in the Moor and pounces on it and destroys the self-made man. For Othello is a warrior and a lover, a slave and a master. Iago is a mischief maker, referred to by W. H. Auden as "the practical joker" (Auden, 1962, p. 246). Yet he is neither comic nor tragic. Iago is a character that had never appeared in ancient Greek and Roman drama. In the context of this vengeful tragedy, how can we explain the presence of Emilia? While she is quite bawdy, she, unlike Othello, seems to have maintained an ego ideal (Freud, 1914c, pp. 67–102) in Desdemona.

Unlike all psychoanalysts, who hold up a mirror to patients' residual childishness in an attempt to work through this, Iago glories in the weaker child and resents its development into a moral being. It is not middle-class morality, but amorality that Iago champions. He is like Alfred Doolittle, who is willing to sell his daughter in George Bernard Shaw's *Pygmalion*.

Iago, like Shakespeare, is a Renaissance man. The expansion of the world that occurred at this time allowed people to expand their own horizons and the horizons of their fantasies. There was suddenly the possibility that creatures feared to be "primitive" would be found—creatures who did not need the state to deter them from destructive acts, and who had no need for the repressive church.

Iago did not have or need progeny. He was entire unto himself. The only human trait that Shakespeare gives him is a wife, who is eventually his undoing, and we suppose it was to terminate an interminable character and an interminable play. No man or woman passes through the developmental shift of helplessness and dependency to autonomy without suffering some residual vulnerabilities. Development is rarely uniform or linear. For instance, witness Julius Caesar and the savage consequences of his archaic dependence, which breaks through to the surface.

Iago is perhaps a proto-Ubermensch of Friedrich Nietzsche. There is no good or bad in Iago. For Nietzsche, the God who suffers or sends his son to suffer is nonsense. Any god that we may devise is an illusion. Freud saw this as well but categorised it as a reaction to the burden of culture (Freud, 1912–1913, pp. 1–161). He settled for Eros and Thanatos (Freud, 1920g, pp. 7–61). Thanatos, the death instinct, is a natural force, which was hard to explain clinically; a force that is counter to love. Iago clearly cannot love but he also cannot hate. Both passions are evidence of the human condition, and to this extent Iago is not human. His actions are arbitrary and unmotivated.

The presence of evil, Iago, seems necessary for the presence of virtue, Desdemona. Virtue, however, is simply the ideal, and the self-deception of the civilised. Evil must always exist and must always win out as evil is the personification of death.

Iago is not a character. He is a primeval force. He is destruction; omniscient, omnipresent, and amorphous. Iago unfuses the sexual and aggressive drives in Othello. He himself is the unfused Thanatos.

Iago is muted but survives in the play. The play is uncomfortable because we are unable to disavow death, and we allow Iago to proceed in his destructiveness and to somehow participate in it with him. The experience of the play leaves us uneasy, but human.

CHAPTER TWO

Mothers in Shakespeare—absent and present

Within William Shakespeare's great body of work, the role of mothers comes as a great surprise. It is tempting to utilise a structuralist's solution. On Shakespeare's stage there were no females. To portray a young woman the solution was simple; to have a boy costumed as a girl. For a man to play an adult woman would be a more difficult dilemma. In a comedy with many adult female characters, such as *The Merry Wives of Windsor*, this would not prove an obstacle. If the costume effect failed, it could simply further the comedic effect. In a tragedy, however, it was more complex. Despite the legal limitations Shakespeare was burdened with, what is of interest is the solution that he chose. We cannot speculate upon the nature of his creative process or the effect his life experience had on his writing. We can, however, examine our reaction to his portrayals of mothers in the resulting artistic creations.

Alan Rothenberg, reflecting on this same paucity of mothers in Shakespeare's dramas, states that "the well-treated, fortunate, happy child is absent as well as the ideal mother, tender, constant, and true, sympathetic alike in the prosperity and adversity … The mother (or nurse) is almost always cold, neglectful, cruel or simply absent physically from the child's emotional hemisphere" (Rothenberg, 1971, pp. 447–468).

In a feminist critique, Janet Adelman sees this absence of mothers as an attempt "to establish masculine identity through the absence of the maternal." Her argument continues: "Shakespeare splits his psychic and dramatic world in two (heterosexual bonds and father–son bonds) isolating its elements from each other and from the maternal body that would be toxic to both" (Adelman, 1992, p. 10). This simultaneously exemplifies the beauty of the projective nature of Shakespeare's work and the subsequent danger of discovering in Shakespeare that which the investigator expects to find. While we firmly believe in separating the author from his work, as in the New Criticism, it is a difficult task. Psychobiography leads only to reductionism. Even Sigmund Freud attempted to resist this view. Freud wrote that: "Before the problem of the creative artist analysis must, alas, lay down its arms" (Freud, 1928b, p. 177). This dictum did not prevent him from using literature to buttress his clinical findings. Yet he was able to also recognise the limitations of psychoanalytic criticism of literature, and delegated it as only one of many ways in increasing our experience of art. It is not what we know or presume to know about Shakespeare, but rather how close reading, hearing, and witnessing the plays allows us to find the Hamlets, Lears, Macbeths, and Falstaffs, in ourselves. Harold Bloom, an aesthetic critic, writes: "we hear, speak and know ourselves and others" (Bloom, 1998, pp. 1–17). We value the insights of creative writers on Shakespeare, such as Samuel Johnson, William Hazlitt, T. S. Eliot, James Joyce, and W. H. Auden, among others. One must be cautious of theorists who attempt to simplify what is complex, and to be wary of formulaic conclusions. Our focus is on our emotional reaction to the works, whatever form this appreciation may take; whether it be love, hate, or any ambivalent combination. Bloom also dislikes socio-historical and political critics and he too understands that Shakespeare's works must speak for themselves. This is most true for this chapter on mothers in Shakespeare, as it is a topic many theorists and critics have deconstructed based upon few assumptions from Shakespeare's own life experience.

We have divided mothers in Shakespeare's plays into four categories: magical mothers, mourning mothers, mothers absent and present.

Magical mothers

In both *The Comedy of Errors* and *The Winter's Tale* Shakespeare either removes the mothers before the play begins or early in the first act. He uses magic to return these absent mothers in the final scene. Both plays utilise a deus ex machina to expel the woman/wife/mother; destroy her by drowning or sudden death, yet restore her to life and to being a central figure in the final act. Unlike simple fantasy, experiments with object permanence, or an oedipal fantasy of destroying the mother, in these plays "real" time must pass—four acts or fifteen years—before the scene of discovery.

In *The Comedy of Errors* Egeon and Emilia have twin sons named Antipholus. The same day they were born, a poor woman had twin boys named Dromio. Egeon purchased these twins for his sons. Soon afterwards, the family suffered a sea storm. Egeon lashed himself to the mast with one Antipholus and one Dromio. Egeon was sure that his wife and the other set of twins had drowned. His remaining son and his companion begin their quest. Each is confronted by mistress or master of the other twin, and they are mistaken for each other. Antipholus of Syracuse falls in love with the sister of the wife of Antipholus of Ephesus. After a further series of mistaken identities they take sanctuary in a nearby priory. The abbess enters with the twins from Syracuse. The family is reunited, and the Abbess reveals that she is Emilia, the wife of Egeon and the mother of the two Antipholus'. *The Comedy of Errors* uses this magical solution in the last act, finding the mother long thought dead, in a convent, after both sons had found wives of their own.

In *The Winter's Tale*, King Polixenes of Bohemia is visiting the court of his dear friend King Leontes of Sicilia. When Polixenes plans to return to Bohemia, Leontes asks his pregnant wife, Hermione, to convince Polixenes to remain, and she is successful. Leontes, surprised that Hermione sways Polixenes so easily, immediately convinces himself that the two are having an affair. Leontes orders Polixenes to be poisoned but Polixenes flees. The Queen gives birth, and Leontes orders this daughter to be left to perish in the wild. The Oracle of Delphi prophesies that Hermione and Polixenes are innocent and that Leontes will have no heir until his lost daughter is found. Leontes' son, Mamillius, has died of a wasting sickness, and Hermione dies, presumably of a broken heart.

A shepherd and his son rescue Hermione's baby and name her Perdita, "the lost little girl". Sixteen years pass and Polixenes' son, Prince Florizel, is betrothed to Perdita, believing her to be a shepherdess. Polixenes orders his son never to see her again. Florizel and Perdita escape to Sicilia where they discover Leontes, still in mourning. The kings reconcile. The company then discover a recently finished statue of Hermione. To everyone's amazement, it is no statue, but Hermione herself, magically restored to life. Unlike *The Comedy of Errors*, in *The Winter's Tale* Hermione is dead. After lost Perdita is found, Hermione comes back to life.

Slights, from any origin, lead to the formation of a simple fantasy in attempt to restore oneself from the pain of this loss. If this fantasy does not hold our experiences and soothe us enough one suffers regression proper. In regression proper the oedipal and pre-oedipal objects (internal representations of people, conflicts and affects from early life) regain their former power. It is as if the emotions associated with the mother are lost and as a result of the regression she can no longer be experienced as a mother or even experienced as human. It is as if she is made of stone. There seems to be something in both *The Winter's Tale* and *The Comedy of Errors* that deal with the regression proper after an unknown slight.

Both plays conclude with coupling. Perdita is engaged, as are the Antipholus twins. It seems marriages must be settled before the mother can return as a full and complete object; real time must pass before the mothers return. It is as if the unconscious and conscious desire for their destruction and ensuing psychotic or melancholic guilt are not worked through in a cathartic manner during the drama itself. This experience leaves the audience to struggle with these issues long after the curtain has fallen.

Absent children

While Lady Macbeth and the Weird Sisters do not belong among our list of mothers, *Macbeth* elucidates some aspects of motherhood and the female struggle for power. Freud attributes Lady Macbeth's murderousness to her barrenness. This is in keeping with Plato's view of fertility and hysteria in *Timaeus*; that the unused womb grows restless and wanders about the body if not utilised "blocking passages, obstructing breathing, and causing disease" (Plato, cited by King, in Gilman, King, Porter, Rousseau, & Showalter, 1993, pp. 3–90).

The Weird Sisters begin the play, introducing us to Macbeth. On the battlefield Macbeth is praised:

> For brave Macbeth—well he deserves that name—
> Disdaining fortune, with his brandish'd steel ... (I.ii.16–17)

King Duncan is pleased with Macbeth for his violence in battle. Macbeth and Banquo wander onto a heath, where the three Weird Sisters present their prophesies, hailing Macbeth as "thane of Glamis" (I.iii.50), "thane of Cawdor" (I.iii.51), and that he "shalt be King hereafter" (I.iii.52). Banquo is told he will father a line of kings, "thou shalt get kings, though thou be none" (I.iii.69). Macbeth wonders if they are women:

> By each at once her choppy finger laying
> Upon her skinny lips: you should be women,
> And yet your beards forbid me to interpret
> That you are so. (I.iii.45–48)

The Weird Sisters are women. They are not aggressive. They function only as an oracle, and seem to only articulate and stir up ambitious fantasies already present in his mind.

Macbeth has been given a new title, Thane of Cawdor. As if by predicting this promotion the Weird Sisters allow Macbeth to consciously fantasise about becoming King. Lady Macbeth, however, suffers none of Macbeth's ambivalence. She is an ambitious woman in a time and in a place when power was sexualised. While Macbeth is a celebrated soldier on the battlefield, he does not manifestly share her quest for power, nor does Lady Macbeth allow him to fantasise. Each time he begins to express some feeling, she rushes to concretise his thoughts into actions. He fantasises about murdering King Duncan, but draws back:

> We will proceed no further in this business.
> He hath honour'd me of late, and I have bought
> Golden opinions from all sorts of people … (I.vii.31–33)

Macbeth is clearly enjoying the King's praise. Lady Macbeth attacks his ambivalence.

> … Art thou afeard
> To be the same in thine own act and valour
> As thou art in desire? Wouldst thou have that
> Which thou esteem'st the ornament of life,
> And live a coward in thine own esteem … (I.vii.40–44)

She makes explicit and merges action with desire, explaining that they should be one and the same, and attacking his mixed feelings as a weakness. She attacks his manhood:

> When you durst do it, then you were a man;
> And to be more than what you were, you would
> Be so much more the man. Nor time nor place
> Did then adhere, and yet you would make both.
> They have made themselves, and that their fitness now
> Does unmake you. (I.vii.49–54)

Lady Macbeth cannot separate fantasy from action. To unmake him is to emasculate him.

Lady Macbeth explains to him that as a woman she is more of a man than he:

> I have given suck, and know
> How tender 'tis to love the babe that milks me:
> I would, while it was smiling in my face,
> Have pluck'd my nipple from his boneless gums,
> And dash'd the brains out, had I so sworn as you
> Have done to this. (I.vii.54–59)

There is no mention of this son. The reference to nursing a baby is all the more striking given that Lady Macbeth has already called to unsex herself and to "take my milk for gall" (I.v.48). She appears to be a woman similar to Volumnia of *Coriolanus*, and perhaps Macbeth is the babe she wishes to nurse, desiring to feed him with ambition rather than milk. Is she the danger of what occurs when a woman has no child or the mother has lost her child?

Macbeth loves the King but simultaneously wants to murder him and take his place. But action is not the solution to his ambivalence when he has not renounced either position. Macbeth stabs the King in his sleep. Suddenly we see his guilt, as Macbeth is hypervigilant and troubled by imagined sounds and hallucinations:

> Is this a dagger which I see before me,
> The handle toward my hand? Come, let me clutch thee.
> I have thee not, and yet I see thee still.
> Art thou not, fatal vision, sensible

> To feeling as to sight? Or art thou but
> A dagger of the mind, a false creation,
> Proceeding from the heat-oppressed brain? (II.i.34–40)

Macbeth expresses the terrible experience of losing one's sense of self. This loss is magnified, as Macbeth needs to maintain his love for the King in order to maintain this image of himself—yet his true feelings towards the King are ambivalent; half of Macbeth loves the King, while the other half wishes to destroy the him:

> Now o'er the one halfworld
> Nature seems dead, and wicked dreams abuse
> The curtain'd sleep. (II.i.50–52)

Lady Macbeth, with her unambivalent, unchecked aggression, takes over. Duncan's sons flee the country. Macbeth is now King.

Lady Macbeth can only be powerful by acting through a man—in this case her husband. She surpasses the Weird Sisters. Macbeth visits the Sisters in attempt to soothe himself. They say:

> … for none of woman born
> Shall harm Macbeth. (IV.i.82–83)

This too is a reference against motherhood, as those who are born from women are described as somehow less powerful. The Weird Sisters themselves form another version of the mother figure; earth goddesses who create a brew of body parts, or as Margaret and Michael Rustin say, with Klienian aesthetics, part objects, to create a "magical production of monster babies" (Rustin & Rustin, 2002, p. 83). They chant:

> Round about the cauldron go;
> In the poison'd entrails throw.
> Toad, that under cold stone
> Days and nights has thirty-one
> Swelter'd venom sleeping got,
> Boil thou first i' the charmed pot. (IV.i.4–9)

Rustin and Rustin read the thirty-one days as a menstrual cycle (2002, pp. 69–94). Macbeth is relieved and asks if Banquo's sons will ever reign in Scotland and the witches' cauldron produces images of spirit boys.

A crowned child holding a tree states that Macbeth will be safe until Great Birnam Wood comes to Dunsinane Hill.

Freed to act, Macbeth sends murderers to slaughter Macduff's wife and children. Macbeth invites Banquo to a royal banquet and hires men to kill him, but his son Fleance escapes. At the banquet, Banquo's ghost enters and sits in Macbeth's place. Macbeth's descent into madness is complete.

Lady Macbeth enters, sleep walking. She tries to wash off imaginary bloodstains from her hands:

> Out, damned spot! out, I say!—One: two: why,
> then, 'tis time to do't.—Hell is murky!—Fie, my
> lord, fie! a soldier, and afeard? What need we
> fear who knows it, when none can call our power to
> account?—Yet who would have thought the old man
> to have had so much blood in him? (V.i.31–36)

Malcolm leads an army against Dunsinane Castle. While encamped in Birnam Wood, the soldiers are ordered to cut down and carry trees as camouflage. Even procreation in the form of trees and nature is destroyed.

Lady Macbeth kills herself. With her death Macbeth is finally free to do what he was unable to do during her lifetime, he is able to identify with her:

> Out, out, brief candle!
> Life's but a walking shadow, a poor player
> That struts and frets his hour upon the stage
> And then is heard no more. It is a tale
> Told by an idiot, full of sound and fury
> Signifying nothing. (V.v.23–28)

Each line foreshadows the imagery of the following line. The candlelight casts a shadow and is extinguished. He uses her language when he says, "Out, out ..." as a way that illustrates his identification with her. This process of identification keeps her alive within him. Macbeth is now less ambivalent about his quest for power.

Macbeth still believes that he has no reason to fear Macduff, for he cannot be killed by any man born of woman. Macduff, speaking of himself in third person, declares:

> Tell thee, Macduff was from his mother's womb
> Untimely ripp'd. (V.viii.15–16)

He is not "of woman born". Macduff kills and beheads Macbeth, thus fulfilling the remaining prophecy. Through Malcolm, order has been restored. In *Macbeth*, we see the result of barrenness or of child loss. The envy in Lady Macbeth has resulted in her murderous fury against men. When she transgresses the laws of hospitality and murders the King while he is a guest in her home, she is doomed and she dies by her own hand.

Absent mothers

There are plays with adult characters that make no mention of the mother, while the father figures prominently, as in *King Lear*. Shakespeare's source for Lear included reference to his queen, yet Shakespeare removed any mention of her. To have no mother on stage is one thing but to expunge these mothers is specific to Shakespeare.

Most of the comedies have no mothers either. In *The Merchant of Venice*, Portia grapples with her father's rules on choosing her husband. Even after his death he is present in the play via the three caskets. There is no mention of her mother. There is an absence of mothers during the youth of these characters. Another example of this occurs in *The Tempest*. This play has special significance for its music, masques, and artistic imagery, as well as for being Shakespeare's final solo work. In its opening scene Prospero asks Miranda of her early life:

> Canst thou remember
> A time before we came unto this cell? (I.ii.38–39)

To which she responds with her earliest memory:

> 'Tis far off,
> And rather like a dream than an assurance
> That my remembrance warrants. Had I not
> Four or five women once that tended me? (I.ii.44–47)

Prospero's narcissistic pleasure of her remembrance of his dukedom eclipses any urge to remind Miranda of any early life with her mother.

Prospero needs her to remind him who he was. Miranda's memory is only of her nursemaids. Certainly Prospero could have easily spoken a line referring to Miranda's lost mother, but he does not.

In *As You Like It* Rosalind's father, Duke Senior, features prominently, as does his brother, Celia's father, Duke Frederick. This play may be seen as a comic mirror to *King Lear*, but it is not only Duke Senior but his entire court that is exiled in the Forest of Arden. There is no mother per se in *Much Ado About Nothing*; Hero's father Leonato has a prominent role yet his wife Innogen, in early editions, was included as a ghost. In *The Two Gentleman of Verona*, Silvia's father, The Duke of Milan, is present but her mother does not appear on stage. There are no mothers in *Love's Labour's Lost* or *Measure for Measure*. In *The Taming of the Shrew*, Kate's father, Baptista Minola, is present but her mother is not. In *A Midsummer Night's Dream* Hermia's father, Egeus, is present but her mother absent. The maternal theme, however, does come to the surface in this drama. Oberon and Titania, the King and Queen of the fairies, use magic to enact their fight over the fate of the changelling. In *Twelfth Night*, Viola and her twin, Sebastian, are orphaned.

Mothers of dead children

There are striking examples of mothers whose young sons are murdered, such as in *King John* and *The Tragedy of King Richard III*. This seems to suggest that the mothers cannot protect the lives of their sons. They all seem to mourn with such rawness that even the murderers find the act of listening to the mother's lament worse than committing the infanticide itself.

In *King John*, the King receives an ambassador from France, who demands, on pain of war, that he renounce his throne in favour of his nephew Arthur, whom the French King, Philip, believes to be the rightful heir. King John orders Hubert to kill Arthur, yet he finds himself unable to do so. Hubert announces that Arthur is dead, but later reveals that Arthur is still alive. King John, delighted, sends him to report the news to the nobles. Meanwhile young Arthur dies, jumping from a castle wall in an attempt to escape his imprisonment. His mother Constance cries over Arthur's death:

> But now will canker-sorrow eat my bud
> And chase the native beauty from his cheek

> And he will look as hollow as a ghost,
> As dim and meagre as an ague's fit,
> And so he'll die; and, rising so again,
> When I shall meet him in the court of heaven
> I shall not know him: therefore never, never
> Must I behold my pretty Arthur more. (III.iv.82–89)

The men in this scene cannot tolerate this mourning, they rush to tidy her hair and to quiet her—not to console, but to stop her. King Philip, who has been fighting to ensure Arthur's place as the rightful heir, replies, "You are as fond of grief as of your child" (III.iv.92).

While we will later discuss *The Tragedy of King Richard III*, focusing on Richard's relationship with his mother, there is, however, a striking scene of Richard's sister-in-law's lament after Richard murders her two sons in the Tower of London. Elizabeth cries:

> Ah, my poor princes! ah, my tender babes!
> My unblown flowers, new-appearing sweets!
> If yet your gentle souls fly in the air
> And be not fix'd in doom perpetual,
> Hover about me with your airy wings,
> And hear your mother's lamentation! (IV.iv.9–14)

Richard attempts to quiet her: "Harp not on that string, madam; that is past" (IV.iv.372). It is not only the murderer who cannot tolerate the child loss; even other mothers try to suppress it. Queen Margaret, a woman who lost an adult son herself, tells Elizabeth she was: "A mother only mock'd with two fair babes …" (IV.iv.87). It seems that mothers who lose their young children have loud complaints that are so primal that their heartbreak is not even addressed to any character or even any deity. While they express outward lamentations, these mothers do not search for nor reach acceptance.

Present mothers

There are three plays where a mother is physically present that deserve special attention: the early drama *The Tragedy of King Richard III*, the *Hamlet* of Shakespeare's maturity, and the later drama of *Coriolanus*.

The Tragedy of King Richard III was written between 1592 and 1593. Friedrich Schiller remarked that it is "one of the most noblest tragedies I know … No Shakespearian play has so much of Greek tragedy" (Schiller, cited in Steiner, 1961, p. 158). Perhaps this comment has to do with his view that King Richard has a tragic flaw. Prior to the action of the play, Queen Margaret was usurped, and her husband and son were murdered at the hands of the brothers of York: Richard, Clarence, and Edward IV. This scenario is one that Richard repeats with various women throughout the play, including his own mother. This relationship between Richard and his mother is stunningly complex.

Richard understands that he is useful as a soldier, and that peace has nothing to offer him. He says of the former soldiers:

> And now,—instead of mounting barbed steeds,
> To fright the souls of fearful adversaries,—
> He capers nimbly in a lady's chamber
> To the lascivious pleasing of a lute.
> But I, that am not shap'd for sportive tricks,
> Nor made to court an amorous looking-glass;
> I, that am rudely stamp'd, and want love's majesty
> To strut before a wanton ambling nymph … (I.i.10–17)

Like Iago, in *Othello*, Richard uses monologues not to reveal something hidden in himself, but rather to seduce the audience. He looks for a mirror in the audience and seduces us with his sadism. He blames his mother, and female nature, as he described himself:

> I, that am curtail'd of this fair proportion,
> Cheated of feature by dissembling nature,
> Deform'd, unfinish'd, sent before my time
> Into this breathing world, scarce half made up … (I.i.18–21)

His mother could not even protect him from the world while in her womb. Richard's deformity, his need to watch his shadow, or to catch his own refection in the glass, is a leitmotif in the play and may attempt to compensate for the lack of the positive maternal. The physical mirror must substitute the mirror function that a child receives from his mother in early life. This establishes a germ of the self, which is elaborated and expanded in the experiences of later life. Richard did not receive or was unable to utilise this mirror function from his mother and seeks it in us, the audience. Richard describes himself:

> And that so lamely and unfashionable
> That dogs bark at me as I halt by them;
> Why, I, in this weak piping time of peace,
> Have no delight to pass away the time,
> Unless to spy my shadow in the sun
> And descant on mine own deformity:
> And therefore, since I cannot prove a lover,
> To entertain these fair well-spoken days,
> I am determined to prove a villain ... (I.i.22–30)

Descant here refers to singing a melody against a fixed harmony; the fixed harmony of his deformity or of his villainy. The only changes that occur during the course of the play are the words he sings, rather than the tune. Richard's brother Clarence stands next in the line of succession:

> Plots have I laid, inductions dangerous,
> By drunken prophecies, libels, and dreams,
> To set my brother Clarence and the King
> In deadly hate, the one against the other ... (I.i.32–35)

Richard, through his manipulation of a soothsayer, has Clarence sent to the Tower of London. While positioning himself to claim the throne there may also be another advantage in destroying his brother—he may be attempting to restore all of their mother's love to himself alone. The true villainy of Richard lies not solely in his agency, but in his ability to read latent murderous desires in others. He recognises Queen Anne's unconscious ambivalence towards her dead husband and capitalises upon it. He seduces Queen Anne as she inters her husband, Richard's nephew, whom he himself has murdered. His body is on the stage during this love scene. Lady Anne curses Richard:

> If ever he have child, abortive be it:
> Prodigious, and untimely brought to light,
> Whose ugly and unnatural aspect
> May fright the hopeful mother at the view,
> And that be heir to his unhappiness. (I.ii.21–25)

Her curse is not that Richard should die, or never love, but rather that he never parent. She wishes her eyes would be "basilisks, to strike thee dead" (I.ii.154). A basilisk is a mythological beast whose reptilian gaze is mortal, much like a male Medusa. Richard says:

> Was ever woman in this humour woo'd?
> Was ever woman in this humour won? (I.ii.232–233)

Lady Anne agrees to marry him. In his monologue Richard tells us that he will discard her once she has served her purpose: "I'll have her; but I will not keep her long" (I.ii.234). Lady Anne will say it was his flattery that caused her to wed him at her husband's burial, disavowing her own participation.

When his seduction of Lady Anne is successful the mirror returns. This time, with pleasure, Richard says:

> Shine out, fair sun, till I have bought a glass,
> That I may see my shadow as I pass. (I.ii.267–268)

Queen Margaret, the widow of Henry VI, returns in defiance of her banishment and warns of Richard:

> … but I do find more pain in banishment
> Than death can yield me here by my abode.
> A husband and a son thou owest to me;
> And thou a kingdom; all of you, allegiance.
> This sorrow that I have by right is yours;
> And all the pleasures you usurp are mine. (I.iii.168–173)

Queen Margaret's injuries are very similar to those of Richard's mother, for she too has lost two sons at Richard's hands. Queen Margaret continues:

> For Edward my son, whichwas Prince of Wales,
> Die in his youth, by like untimely violence.
> Thyself, a queen, for me that was a queen,
> Outlive thy glory like my wretched self:
> Long mayst thou live to wail thy children's loss …
> (I.iii.200–204)

Again Richard is cursed as if he is a parent. Yet, in Richard's plotting to become king, with all his detailed machinations, there is no thought of offspring.

Richard orders Clarence's murder. Clarence relates a dream to his jailer:

> Methoughts I saw a thousand fearful wrecks;
> Ten thousand men that fishes gnaw'd upon;
> Wedges of gold, great anchors, heaps of pearl,
> Inestimable stones, unvalu'd jewels,
> All scatter'd in the bottom of the sea.
> Some lay in dead men's skulls, and in those holes
> Where eyes did once inhabit, there were crept—
> As 'twere in scorn of eyes–reflecting gems,
> That woo'd the slimy bottom of the deep,
> And mock'd the dead bones that lay scatter'd by. (I.iv.24–33)

The many murders in this play and Richard's glee in performing them seem to desensitise us to the violence, and we participate in it with him. In contrast, Clarence's dream of skeletons and jewels populating the bottom of the sea pulls us back through his poetic image of death. He thus reminds us of the true tragic finitude of life.

Clarence pleads with the murderers, and tells them his brother will reward them better for his life than Edward will for his death. Clarence does not believe his brother ordered his execution.

Richard uses the news of Clarence's unexpected death to send Edward IV, his last brother, to his deathbed, positioning the Queen to appear responsible for Clarence's execution. The death of Edward IV leaves Richard as Protector. He meets his nephew while en route to his coronation. Richard convinces the young prince and his brother to seek refuge in the Tower of London. Richard now has no impediments and mounts a campaign as the true heir to the throne.

He has his nephews in the tower murdered and he poisons Lady Anne. As we have discussed earlier, Queen Elizabeth mourns the princes' deaths. She asks Queen Margaret's help in cursing. Richard asks Queen Elizabeth to help him win her daughter's hand in marriage, and Elizabeth demurs. She is the first character to refuse him. Richard's mother, the Duchess of York, distances herself from Richard.

> O ill-dispersing wind of misery!
> O my accursed womb, the bed of death!
> A cockatrice hast thou hatch'd to the world,
> Whose unavoided eye is murderous. (IV.i.52–55)

A cockatrice is a mythological creature born from the egg of a cock and incubated by a reptile. The Duchess here projects her own villainy onto Richard, even at his conception. It is an evil she cannot see in herself. She describes her womb as if it were an independent object and not her own. The Duchess of York says:

> He is my son—yea, and therein my shame;
> Yet from my dugs he drew not this deceit. (II.ii.27–28)

She cannot recognise herself in him or the usefulness this disavowal offers her. The Duchess continues:

> I have bewept a worthy husband's death,
> And lived by looking on his images;
> But now two mirrors of his princely semblance
> Are crack'd in pieces by malignant death,
> And I for comfort have but one false glass
> That grieves me when I see my shame in him. (II.ii.49–54)

The deformity of her child represents something terrible in her; that she has produced one of the most villainous characters in all creation. The Duchess describes her experience of being Richard's mother, and it is obvious that she has complicated feelings towards him:

> A grievous burthen was thy birth to me;
> Tetchy and wayward was thy infancy;
> Thy school-days frightful, desperate, wild and furious;
> Thy prime of manhood daring, bold, and venturous;
> Thy age confirm'd, proud, subdued, bloody, treacherous
> More mild, but yet more harmful, kind in hatred:
> What comfortable hour canst thou name
> That ever graced me in thy company? (IV.iv.168–175)

She explains how Richard was as an accessory to her; to her wishes and to her disappointments. Ironically it is Richard who describes the young prince as just like his mother from "head to toe" and recognises the mother-son bond. When Elizabeth confronts Richard he replies:

> But in your daughter's womb I bury them:
> Where, in that nest of spicery, they shall breed
> Selves of themselves, to your recomforture. (IV.iv.422–424)

Richard recognises that children can function for the mother as "selves of themselves".

The Duchess of York is not aware of the usefulness Richard's aggression holds for her or the deformed part of her character that it manifests. She conjures the image that her tears will drown the world. Perhaps this is the ocean that first appeared in Clarence's dream. *The Tragedy of King Richard III*, with its many animal references, rivals only *King Lear* in its primitive animalism. Here the war-torn country is the deformed body of a woman:

> This noble isle doth want her proper limbs;
> Her face defaced with scars of infamy,
> Her royal stock graft with ignoble plants,
> And almost shoulder'd in the swallowing gulf
> Of blind forgetfulness and dark oblivion. (III.vii.123–127)

It is not only the disease of their world but the death of motherhood. Richard's final scene is foreshadowed by his mother, as the Duchess of York says of her sons:

> Clean over-blown, themselves, the conquerors,
> Make war upon themselves; brother to brother,
> Blood to blood, self against self … (II.iv.58–60)

Richard here struggles for a consistent self without maternal ties. Richard does not talk about his need for an heir nor does he seem to expect to have a child to inherit his throne. Richard exists only in the present moment.

Richard faces rebellions. He is visited by the ghosts of his victims. Each recalls how Richard has murdered them and each asks that he think about them during his battle. He wonders:

> What do I fear? Myself? There's none else by.
> Richard loves Richard: that is, I am I.
> Is there a murderer here? No. Yes, I am:
> Then fly. What, from myself? Great reason why—
> Lest I revenge. What, myself upon myself?
> Alack, I love myself. Wherefore? For any good
> That I myself have done unto myself?
> O, no! Alas, I rather hate myself
> For hateful deeds committed by myself.
> I am a villain. Yet I lie, I am not.
> Fool, of thyself speak well. Fool, do not flatter.
> My conscience hath a thousand several tongues,
> And every tongue brings in a several tale,
> And every tale condemns me for a villain.
> Perjury, perjury, in the highest degree,
> Murder, stern murder, in the direst degree … (V.iii.183–198)

In this beautiful passage the ambivalence of Richard comes through as if he is two separate people. With this ambivalence Richard hardly puts up a fight. Although he does not live well, dying becomes him and he thus embraces his death.

At the battle of Bosworth Field, Lord Stanley and his followers desert Richard's side, whereupon Richard calls for the execution of Lord Stanley's son. Richard is left unhorsed upon the field. Richmond kills Richard. Richmond succeeds to the throne as Henry VII and marries Princess Elizabeth from the House of York.

Mother in Hamlet

Freud himself contrasted *Hamlet* to *Oedipus Rex*. For Oedipus, the play begins after his infamous deeds are already completed. It is his insistence on discovering the truth that prompts the action of the play, rather than the deeds themselves. Freud considered the name the Hamlet complex, but it is no surprise that he chose *Oedipus* over *Hamlet*, as Freud himself struggled throughout his life with a need to know.

The tripartite model is composed of the id, ego, and superego. The id is composed of instinctual drives and pleasure-seeking motivations, the ego regulates these drives and is an interface between them and the external world, and the superego is an internalisation of parental values or conscience that is to control the instincts of the oedipal phase (Freud, 1923b, pp. 12–66). Although this tripartite process is clearly present in *Hamlet*, Hamlet the character is many ways before and beyond Freud in terms of his psychological understanding of life. Hamlet begins the play using what he is not to understand who he is. He is a young student, who has already had a dalliance with Ophelia of whom he speaks of as a sexual object. However, he is an intellectual boy with more interest in books than women, war, or the affairs of state.

As the audience, we long for this to be a play of vengeance, and *Hamlet* is often compared to *The Spanish Tragedy*; structurally this coupling is just. But *Hamlet* is more a play about the relationship between an adult son searching for identifications with his father and stepfather. The sexualisation of Gertrude seems to be a marker in his development. By Act V the gravedigger refers to Hamlet as thirty; ten years have passed since the play's opening. Hamlet had an interrupted mourning, and incomplete identification with his father at the time of his father's death, and as he grows closer to his father's age when he died, Hamlet's mourning and identification grow more complicated. Hamlet then embarks on a lifelong quest to search for the missing piece within himself that was murdered along with his father. Hamlet's dilemma is that he shared only a name with his father; the two were different in all other aspects. Hamlet is then left with only a stepfather:

> My father's brother—but no more like my father
> Than I to Hercules. (I.ii.152–153)

After meeting his father's ghost, Hamlet exclaims:

> My fate cries out
> And makes each petty artery in this body
> As hardy as the Nemean lion's nerve. (I.iv.81–83)

The Nemean lion was, of course, Hercules' first labour. It is interesting that Hamlet likens himself both to Hercules and to Hercules' first adversary. By Act V Hamlet says to Laertes, "Let Hercules himself do what he may ..." (V.i.286). Hercules is thus no longer a part of his imago. This may represent, through the process of the drama, the development of the conflictual identification with Claudius and King Hamlet.

When King Hamlet's ghost enters, Horatio describes him "with fear and wonder" (I.i.47), in his "fair and warlike form" (I.i.50), dressed as a warrior, with the:

> ... very armour he had on
> When he the ambitious Norway combated ... (I.i.63–64)

There is a lusty exchange with Horatio, when Horatio asks the ghost if he has returned for treasure "in the womb of the earth" (I.i.141). Here Horatio imagines the earth as a female in which men bury "extorted treasure".

Hamlet will not yet take in Claudius as a father, nor will he fully take in the ghost of his father as substitute. Hamlet says to the ghost:

> Be thou a spirit of health or goblin damn'd,
> Bring with thee airs from heaven or blasts from hell ...
> (I.iv.40–41)

During the Middle Ages it was a common belief that if one had a vision one had to be very careful that it was not Satan putting on a disguise. This superstition persists to this day in the Catholic Church. Horatio advises Hamlet:

> What if it tempt you toward the flood, my lord
> Or to the dreadful summit of the cliff. (I.iv.69–70)

The ghost's effect on Hamlet may be far worse than Horatio imagines, as the ghost interferes with Hamlet's identification with his mother, with Claudius, and with what little he had identified with his father in life. What is left to identify with, however, is only the deadness in the father's ghost, not the father himself.

The preoccupation with death that permeates Hamlet has to do with the awareness that he himself is already dead. Bloom, citing Nietzsche, states that words come when feelings are dead (Bloom, 1998, pp. 383–431). Hamlet's cleverness and irreverent witticisms are ways to

> worm is your only emperor for diet: we fat all
> creatures else to fat us, and we fat ourselves for
> maggots: your fat king and your lean beggar is but
> variable service, two dishes, but to one table:
> that's the end. (IV.iii.18–24)

Hamlet is a modern man with no hope for heaven or hell. To Claudius, Hamlet says:

> A man may fish with the worm that hath eat of a
> king, and eat of the fish that hath fed of that worm.
> (IV.iii.27–28)

To which Claudius responds: "What dost you mean by this?" (IV.iii.29). Hamlet answers:

> Nothing but to show you how a king may go a
> progress through the guts of a beggar. (IV.iii.30–31)

This is not to threaten Claudius, it is simply the view of Hamlet's minimally cathected world. In wondering about life Hamlet muses:

> ... and indeed it goes so heavily
> with my disposition that this goodly frame, the
> earth, seems to me a sterile promontory, this most
> excellent canopy, the air, look you, this brave
> o'erhanging firmament, this majestical roof fretted
> with golden fire, why, it appears no other thing to
> me than a foul and pestilent congregation of vapours.
> (II.ii.297–303)

> ... And yet, to me,
> what is this quintessence of dust? man delights not
> me: no, nor woman neither, though by your smiling
> you seem to say so. (II.ii.308–311)

When he visits the graveyard in Act V he is talked about in the third person by the gravedigger, furthering the sensation that he himself is a ghost haunting his own grave. Hamlet is already dead.

When we first encounter Queen Gertrude she is King Claudius' soft echo. Gruffly, Claudius requests that Hamlet leave his studies and remain in Denmark. We are unsure of the motivation of this request and, Gertrude interrupts our thoughts:

> Let not thy mother lose her prayers, Hamlet.
> I pray thee stay with us, go not to Wittenberg. (I.ii.118–119)

Gertrude is again the seductive echo to Rosencrantz and Guildenstern when she gently appeals to their narcissism:

> Good gentlemen, he hath much talk'd of you;
> And sure I am two men there are not living
> To whom he more adheres. (II.ii.19–21)

She strikes us as flattering, yet clear headed. While Claudius plots with Polonius, Ophelia, Rosencrantz, and Guildenstern as to why Hamlet is mad, Gertrude suggests plainly and to the point:

> I doubt it is no other but the main
> His father's death and our o'erhasty marriage. (II.ii.57–58)

Shakespeare's main source for *Hamlet* was an Ur—Hamlet, an earlier play in which the young prince feigned madness to protect himself from being killed. Shakespeare takes this piece of the plot but loses the reason: there is no rival for Hamlet's accession. Hamlet is next in line for his father's throne, to which Claudius offers:

> … And with no less nobility of love
> Than that which dearest father bears his son
> Do I impart toward you. (I.ii.110–112)

Has there ever been an accession offered with such ease? Queen Gertrude may be guilty of marrying her husband's brother hastily, but we never quite know how much she knows of Claudius' guilt. After Hamlet produces his play re-enacting the murder scene, the King orders it to be stopped. When Hamlet cannot keep himself from asking Gertrude her reaction, she replies clearly, "The lady doth protest too much, methinks" (III.ii.225). This is not the response of a conspirator, but of a queen who sees her hasty remarriage as a simple action requiring little to "protest" or even to think about. Unlike Hamlet, Gertrude is not introspective. Is it a vengeance ploy, or palpable glee when Rosencrantz tells Hamlet that his mother liked his play, Hamlet replies, "O wonderful son, that can so astonish a mother!" (III.ii.318)? This response feels like one of pride rather than one of sarcasm.

Hamlet describes his parents' marriage in idealistic terms:

> ... why, she would hang on him
> As if increase of appetite had grown
> By what it fed on ... (I.ii.143–145)

This appetite that grows by eating will be reinvented in *Coriolanus*. The ghost does not return as a wronged soldier, or solely a murdered man, but also as a jealous husband. He says to Hamlet:

> Let not the royal bed of Denmark be
> A couch for luxury ... (I.v.82–83)

Here the ghost is stirring up Hamlet's sexual feelings towards his mother. He is not a soldier but a thinker, he says: "I will speak daggers to her, but use none" (III.ii.387). Hamlet places Gertrude in front of a mirror so she can "see herself". But it is Hamlet who misuses the mirror. What Hamlet sees in the mirror is Polonius, and then murders him. Gertrude sees herself in the mirror; it is Hamlet who cannot see himself. After this first murder, Hamlet seems more like Claudius or his father's ghost, and he sees Gertrude as more sexualised after initially denying her sexuality and telling the Queen:

> You cannot call it love; for at your age
> The heyday in the blood is tame, it's humble,
> And waits upon judgment ... (III.iv.68–70)

Now Hamlet makes it explicit, likening her sexuality to that of animals:

> ... Nay, but to live
> In rank sweat of an enseamed bed,

> Stew'd in corruption, honeying and making love
> Over the nasty sty! (III.iv.91–94)

The ghost interrupts, as if both Hamlet and the ghost are overstimulated by Gertrude's bedchamber. The ghost warns Hamlet, "Do not forget" (III.iv.110). The visitation is the vengeance on Claudius, but the ghost interrupts at the very moment Gertrude becomes a sexualised object for Hamlet. He can identify with his dead father as a dead soldier, or he can he can remain alive and identify with him through his love of Gertrude. Hamlet only fences with words, not swords. Gertrude is lost, she entreats Hamlet, "What shall I do?" (III.iv.182), to which Hamlet, strengthened by the murder he committed, reiterates his earlier comment, "But go not to mine uncle's bed" (III.iv.161), with a more descriptive, fantasised prohibition:

> Not this, by no means, that I bid you do:
> Let the bloat king tempt you again to bed;
> Pinch wanton on your cheek; call you his mouse;
> And let him, for a pair of reechy kisses,
> Or paddling in your neck with his damn'd fingers …
> (III.iv.183–187)

Gertrude's seductive interactions with Hamlet make her the most-often cited mother in Shakespeare's works, but she holds a marginal role in this play. Claudius has his own guilt that needs not be projected, describing it as "Oh, heavy burthen" (III.i.54), and ponders the deed:

> What if this cursed hand
> Were thicker than itself with brother's blood,
> Is there not rain enough in the sweet heavens
> To wash it white as snow? (III.iii.43–46)

Sounding for a moment like Lady Macbeth, he quickly recovers himself, bargaining out loud:

> My crown, mine own ambition, and my queen.
> May one be pardon'd and retain th' offence? (III.iii.55–56)

Unlike Laertes, Hamlet does not rush to revenge. Perhaps even Hamlet recognises that Claudius, too, is his father; a cowardly one, but one he more resembles. For Laertes, this is a drama of vengeance in the Greek style. In contrast with Hamlet, Laertes confronts the king the instant he hears of his father's death:

> O thou vile king,
> Give me my father. (IV.v.115–116)

Claudius in turn baits Laertes:

> … Was your father dear to you?
> Or are you like the painting of a sorrow,
> A face without a heart? (IV.vii.106–108)

This is, of course, for Claudius' own ends, to set Laertes against Hamlet. Identification seems to flow in both directions. It is interesting that Claudius, a man of action, interrupts his planning and says, "Let's further think of this … ." (IV.vii.148), for it is Hamlet who is king in the land of thought.

> Yet, this is not a play of vengeance. Hamlet says to the ghost:
> Haste me to know't, that I with wings as swift
> As meditation or the thought of love
> May sweep to my revenge. (I.v.29–31)

This is Hamlet's play, not a Greek tragedy of action. Hamlet does not swiftly seek revenge. Instead he learns about himself and therefore develops. When offered opportunities for vengeance, Hamlet appears to let them slip. After the "Mousetrap", the play within the play, Claudius acts the guilty part to which Hamlet responds: "Swounds, I should take it: for it cannot be …" (II.ii.572). His anger shifts quickly, however, from Claudius to Gertrude, to his father's Ghost, and back to himself. Hamlet finds himself alone with Claudius and draws his sword, but is unable to murder him. Hamlet intellectualises that he should not kill while Claudius is praying because then he would go to heaven, not that he believes it. Hamlet would rather wait until Claudius is "in th' incestuous pleasure of his bed" (III.iii.90).

In Act IV Hamlet can only refer to vengeance as to "spur my dull revenge" (IV.iv.33). By Act V, only when the Queen is murdered by Claudius can Hamlet murder Claudius and then suicide. The end of mothers is the end of the world when Hamlet says to Ophelia:

> Get thee to a nunnery: why wouldst thou be a
> breeder of sinners? (III.i.121–122)

He is now so fixated on Gertrude he has no feeling for Ophelia except anger, and he knows the dangers of women. Hamlet continues:

> If thou dost marry, I'll give thee this plague for
> thy dowry: be thou as chaste as ice, as pure as
> snow, thou shalt not escape calumny. (III.i.135–137)

For Hamlet, to have tender feelings towards Ophelia will undo him and he will need to acknowledge feelings that he has towards Gertrude and his fathers, because it would bring him back to living. Hamlet says:

> I'll no more on't; it hath
> made me mad. I say, we will have no more marriages:
> those that are married already, all but one, shall
> live; the rest shall keep as they are. (III.i.148–151)

Without marriage and procreation the world ends. The oedipal situation is cyclical and life-enhancing—to avoid it consciously or unconsciously there are no objects and the cycle ceases.

Coriolanus is thought to have been written between 1607 and 1608. Unlike Hamlet, Coriolanus is all action and little thought. He is an imperious patrician with a marked inability to compromise, even to get the power that he seems to seek. He is described as a war-machine, murderous and brave. What else can we expect with a mother who sent him off to battle at sixteen with the admonition to come back with scars or not at all? Both *Coriolanus* and *The Tragedy of King Richard III* illustrate a specific type of mother relation with an adult son. Both Volumnia and the Duchess of York use their sons to function as an aspect of themselves. For Volumnia this is an ego syntonic action, as the aggression and murderous rage on which she nurses Coriolanus is a diet of which she is keenly aware, but unable to access as a woman. We see minimal struggle within this single-minded character.

The play opens as the people are starving; deprived of corn by their government, they are angry and mistrustful, like hungry children whose cries its government-parents do not recognise. From the very beginning of the play the citizens understand that the warrior Martius is brave, less for the sake of Rome, but rather that he:

> ... did it to
> please his mother. (I.i.37–38)

When we first encounter Martius' mother Volumnia she is discussing the interchangeability between son and husband, sex and aggressivity. She says:

> ... If my son were my husband I
> should freelier rejoice in that absence wherein he
> won honour, than in the embracements of his bed, where
> he would show most love. (I.iii.2–5)

She continues to startle us with a quality not unlike listening to an interview with a mother of a terrorist who glories in her son's death with the phallic quality of the rage of a devalued woman. Volumnia says:

> had I had a dozen sons, each in my love
> alike, and none less dear than thine and my good
> Martius, I had rather had eleven die nobly for their
> country, than one voluptuously surfeit out of action. (I.i.23–26)

Here Volumnia would rather her child dead than a coward. Perhaps it is because, husbandless, her son is the only access to power and aggressivity available to her. She says:

> ... The breasts of Hecuba
> When she did suckle Hector, look'd not lovelier
> Than Hector's forehead when it spit forth blood
> At Grecian sword contemning. (I.iii.41–44)

She likens death blood of a child to breast milk, favouring to look upon the former.

When Martius returns from battle, his mother responds to the injury, when she says: "O, he is wounded; I thank the gods for't" (II.i.120). In like fashion he brags about mothers "that lack sons" (II.i.179) on account of his feats of killing. Shakespeare often gives us hints at the origin of villainy, as in the deformed shape of Richard III, and Iago's rivalry with Othello. Here it is as if Shakespeare cannot say often enough that Martius kills just to kill. Cominius comments:

> ... he covets less
> Than misery itself would give, rewards
> His deeds with doing them, and is content
> To spend the time to end it. (II.ii.126–129)

In recognition of his great courage, Cominius gives Caius Martius the agnomen of Coriolanus. Martius here becomes his name, anticipated by the title.

When his name is changed, Coriolanus' mother encourages him to run for consul. Coriolanus is hesitant to do this, but he bows to his mother's wishes. He is offered as consul by the senate and with this he seems to unravel. He cannot be politic with the citizens he describes as: "the mutable, rank-scented meinie" (III.i.66). It is not a character change, but rather a static character facing a change in the surroundings. He is at home at war, but there is no place for him at peace. Menenius mistakes this rigid identification with his mother as nobility, which Coriolanus is unable to flatter. It is something more primitive than that.

Faced with opposition, the warrior Coriolanus flies into a rage and rails against the concept of popular rule. He compares allowing plebeians to have power over the patricians to allowing "crows to peck the eagles" (III.i.140). The two tribunes condemn Coriolanus as a traitor for his words, and order him to be banished. Coriolanus retorts that it is he who banishes Rome from his presence. He is not even aware of the conflict within himself, even as it leads him to his banishment.

Volumnia speaks of this identification when she tells Coriolanus:

> I have a heart as little apt as yours,
> But yet a brain that leads my use of anger
> To better vantage. (III.ii.30–32)

When Coriolanus loses his power in Rome, Volumnia begins to disintegrate. She says: "Thy valiantness was mine, thou suck'dst it from me ..." (III.ii.130). It is Volumnia, not Coriolanus, who has developed during the course of the play, as we witness her change and her fall. After his exile and the loss of her warrior self she says:

> Anger's my meat: I sup upon myself
> And so shall starve with feeding. (IV.ii.50–51)

These words could have been uttered by Coriolanus as an infant; he was fed valiantness and murderousness instead of breast milk, and in searching for more of his mother's poisoned milk, so he did starve himself to his murder.

Coriolanus' aggressiveness is normalised when he is a soldier and only in peacetime does his one-dimensionality come forth. Volumnia is fed on anger throughout the play. Prior to his exile she seems gorgon-like, yet afterwards she appears appropriate—as her anger is no longer free-floating and has an object to rest upon. No longer diffuse, she is angry at something.

When he sees his mother bowing before him, Coriolanus says:

> My mother bows,
> As if Olympus to a molehill should
> In supplication nod … (V.iii.29–31)

This is perhaps the only line in which he sounds human, as he reveals his identification, idealisation, and devaluation of himself. Interestingly, Menenius says of Coriolanus:

> … there is no more mercy
> in him than there is milk in a male tiger … (V.iv.28–29)

It is true that Coriolanus has no mercy, and this reference again to mothers' milk reminds us that Volumnia is the impossibility—the female tiger bearing male murderousness.

After being exiled from Rome, Coriolanus seeks out Aufidius and offers to let Aufidius kill him in order to revenge the country that had banished him. Instead, Coriolanus leads a new assault on Rome. Volumnia pleads with her son to spare the city:

> Making the mother, wife and child to see
> The son, the husband and the father, tearing
> His country's bowels out. (V.iii.101–103)

Volumnia has never before requested that he choose peace. To spare the city he has fled condemns him to death. If he acquiesces to her wishes the Volsces will kill him. He is unable to rebel against her. His self is merged with hers. Her destruction would kill him just as much as his own death. The self *vs.* the self here has no resolution. Both are aspects of one self, and both are equal dangers. Volumnia again uses the language of the body to plead with him:

> March to assault thy country than to tread—
> Trust to't, thou shalt not—on thy mother's womb
> That brought thee to this world. (V.iii.123–125)

She tells him that she will suicide if he does not obey her. For Coriolanus, his own death is preferable to matricide. Volumnia succeeds in dissuading her son from destroying Rome, and Coriolanus instead concludes a peace treaty between the Volscians and the Romans. When Coriolanus returns to the Volscian capital, conspirators, organised by Aufidius, kill him for his betrayal. In this final act of hers she undoes him, and we experience its inevitability. It is a part that must be played out by Coriolanus, even to his very destruction. In exile, Coriolanus asks if only a man could be "author of himself", rather than a character in someone else's play; in his case, a character in his mother's drama. But this is an impossibility, particularly in the realm of relationships. We are always actors in others' dramas and they in ours. This line represents one of the most significant differences between Coriolanus and King Richard III, as Richard prides himself not only on being his own "author" but also the author of other characters' unspoken or unconscious desires. Perhaps a significant difference between the two mothers is that Volumnia had use for Coriolanus no matter how self-serving, while the Duchess of York could not tolerate the role that Richard acted out for her.

Conclusion

Like Hamlet, we are at times stage directors, moving from Aristotle and Anna O's view of catharsis alone, with its "as if" quality towards Shakespearian character development. The Duchess of York, for instance, asks why calamity should be "full of words" (IV.iv.126) to which Queen Elizabeth replies:

> Let them have scope: though what they do impart
> Help not all, yet do they ease the heart. (IV.iv.130–131)

We began this chapter searching Shakespeare's works to further elucidate mother characters in his dramas. What we found is somewhat different from what we were seeking. We cannot say that there is a difference in the mother role in comedies, tragedies, or the history plays, nor can we elucidate a theme based upon different phases of Shakespeare's career. Why there are so few mother relationships in these plays remains a mystery; those that do appear are rich, strange, and complex.

CHAPTER THREE

Disguise and disavowal in *The Merchant of Venice* and *Romeo and Juliet*

A ristotle defined tragedy as "… an imitation of an action that is complete and whole and of a certain magnitude. A whole is that which has a beginning and middle and an end" (Aristotle, 335 BCE, p. 14). Tragedy is first defined as an external event that occurs outside of the individual and can clearly be observed by the audience. A man cannot be a tragic hero, however, until he himself can identify the root of his own downfall. For Aristotle, the second component of tragedy is that this external event of action must also have a limited corollary in the internal world of the hero, who is able to recognise that he himself brought these events to pass. Elizabethan and Jacobean drama developed out of the passion plays of the English church and is not a descendant of Greek and Roman drama. The Elizabethans and Jacobeans, led by William Shakespeare and his contemporaries, had a very different conception of tragedy. Shakespeare, for the first time in the English language, relocated the action of tragedy from the external world to the internal world. Recognising one's culpability was no longer enough to define a tragic hero. Now tragedy is recognised as an internal process, rather than simply one of action. It seems tragedy is when the hero requires that others respond to him in a specific manner. This need, this insistence, and interference with it forms tragedy. Thus tragedy is shifted from an individual's phenomena to an interactive two-person psychology. Additionally, Shakespeare supplies us with many "heroes" within each play, as these internal conflicts are no longer limited to the tragic hero, but affect the internal world of most characters of the histories, tragedies, and even the pure comedies. The characters' reactions, solutions and attempted solutions to these conflicts are as varied as the patients we see in our consulting rooms. The depth of the characters does not change between the genres. A comic character suffers the same magnitude as a tragic one. The distinction between comedy and tragedy, then, is no longer a tragic flaw and self-actualisation but rather it is only the difference in how the conflicts are solved. Traditionally, the distinction between comedy and tragedy has been conceptualised in their resolution, as comedies end in marriage and tragedies end in death. However it is more accurate to say that it is the manner in which these conflicts are addressed, worked through, overlooked or resolved that truly categorises each play. For Aristotle, tragedy was the result of a character flaw of hubris, and an attempt to take aspects of the gods for oneself. Comedy concludes in magical solutions, and tragedy concludes with insolvable conflicts. By this definition *The Merchant of Venice* is a comedy. Despite the suffering of Antonio and Shylock, its rash love, and disguised meetings, it ends with the consummation of three marriages, and all characters either get what they need from the other or characters abandon or disavow this need. *Romeo and Juliet*, written the same year, is a tragedy, although it contains similar conflicts. The characters' needs cannot be abandoned or sublimated. The gilded statues of the dead lovers underscores that there is no possibility for a new beginning. In both genres the characters need another—in comedies this occurs, in tragedies the others are unable or unwilling. In the tragedies the characters insist others react, needing someone to act or be a certain way, and the true tragedy occurs when this is interfered with. It is no longer self-actualisation that defines the depth of the tragic hero. Instead, Shakespeare's characters are left with a lack of understanding of their contributions, and the focus has shifted from self-awareness to that which one receives or is withheld from others.

The Merchant of Venice is a curious play in that it has not entirely sustained itself as it was written. While remaining true to the script, the comic role of Shylock has been transformed into that of a tragic character. The play can only be a comedy if we embrace the anti-Jewish sentiment of the late 1500s to which Shakespeare was pandering.

This is something that subsequent audiences have struggled to do. As early as 1709 Nicholas Rowe noted that he was uncomfortable witnessing Shylock as a comic figure (Brown, 1955, p. xxxiv). One hundred years later Edmund Kean's performance had assumed a more tragic form, and William Hazlitt said "that certainly our sympathies are much oftener with him than his enemies" (Hazlitt, 1814, pp. 276–277). One is tempted to think of it as Shylock's play and not Antonio's. While Shylock was simply a stock comic character in repertoire at that time, his role has become so prestigious over the generations that it has been played by Sir Henry Irving, Sir Laurence Olivier, Sir Michael Redgrave, and Sir John Gielgud. Of the play, Harold Bloom simply wrote that he wished Shakespeare had never written it (Bloom, 1998, pp. 171–191). The title is *The Merchant of Venice* and Antonio is that merchant. Act I begins with Antonio's melancholy:

> In sooth I know not why I am so sad,
> It wearies me, you say it wearies you … (I.i.1–2)

Antonio describes his friends' empathic position of sharing his pain, yet qualifies it with "you say it wearied you". Perhaps he is not convinced, or is unable to utilise their empathy:

> But how I caught it, found it, or came by it,
> What stuff 'tis made of, whereof it is born,
> I am to learn:
> And such a want-wit sadness makes of me,
> That I have much ado to know myself. (I.i.3–7)

Melancholia, for Antonio and his friends, is not simply caused by the excess of black bile. Shakespeare not only surpasses the humours, but he actually describes a true anaclitic depression. It is hard to reconcile this successful and popular merchant to his impoverished and almost objectless state. Salerio and Solanio suggest the cause is his sea ventures: "Your mind is tossing on the ocean" (I.i.8). Attempting to make Antonio feel better by giving his feeling state a name, Salerio continues that if it were himself he would perseverate upon the ships:

> Should I go to church
> And see the holy edifice of stone
> And not bethink me straight of dangerous rocks … (I.i.29–31)

Salerio describes always associating what one is concerned about—one's reality—where everything is reinterpreted. The causation changes. Association takes on meanings of his central concerns, namely his ships. Solanio tries his hand by suggesting: "Why, then you are in love" (I.i.46). Antonio denies this. He resembles a man in mourning. Gratiano says:

> You look not well, Signior Antonio,
> You have too much respect upon the world:
> They lose it that do buy it with much care;-
> Believe me, you are marvellously chang'd. (I.i.73–76)

Gratiano, with metaphor of selling and buying, uses the language of merchants and commerce. It seems that Antonio is losing attachment or cathexis to the external world. Antonio explains:

> I hold the world but as the world, Gratiano,
> A stage, where every many must play a part,
> And mine a sad one. (I.i.77–79)

Antonio has little interest in the world, his sea ventures do not trouble him and there is a timelessness to Antonio's state. Lorenzo says accurately:

> My Lord Bassanio, since you have found Antonio
> We two will leave you ... (I.i.69–70)

Despite being unable to name the source of Antonio's sadness, the friends understand that once joined by Bassanio it is time for them to depart. This is one's hope for Antonio. His attachment to Bassanio seems to tether Antonio to the world.

These characters understand Antonio has strong feelings for the young, reckless Bassanio. *The Merchant of Venice* was based on *Il Pecorone*, by Giovanni Fiorentino (Fiorentino, reprinted in Brown, 1955, pp. 140–152). In this, Antonio is the godfather to Bassanio, thus easily explaining Antonio's love and devotion. While remaining fairly close to this source, Shakespeare deviates from the original. Antonio is not Bassanio's godfather and Shakespeare removes any obvious, external explanation for Antonio's devotion to the self-serving

Bassanio. Bassanio is the only character who takes no notice of Antonio's mood.

Bassanio uses merchant language of searching for that of value in his metaphors. This proves to be the language of Venice. The profit motive infiltrates the prose and the poetry. This Venice is one of illusion in which ships magically return replenished with spices and silks.

Antonio immediately needs to bask in the light of Bassanio's affect. Antonio almost begs Bassanio to tell him of his excitement.

The intensity of this request is Antonio's need to experience something vicariously via Bassanio. Knowing he represents something to Antonio, Bassanio seductively asks to borrow more money. Antonio cares not that Bassanio asks for money and feels pressure to supply it to him. Bassanio is a love object for Antonio, and Antonio therefore needs Bassanio for his own survival. Antonio is attempting to utilise Bassanio's happiness in place of his own. Bassanio does not recognise this in him. Antonio replies to this continuous request:

> My purse, my person, my extremest means
> Lie all unlock'd to your occasions. (I.i.137–138)

When Bassanio attempts to justify how it will be repaid, Antonio stops him and asks him only:

> You know me well, and herein spend but time
> To wind about my love with circumstance,
> And out of doubt you do me now more wrong
> In making question of my uttermost
> Than if you had made waste of all I have … (I.i.153–157)

Antonio explains to Bassanio that he can take everything. Antonio may be looking for a rationalisation to destroy himself and would happily lay waste to himself for Bassanio's sake. It is beyond generosity and illustrates the masochistic quality and emphasises Antonio's feeling of Bassanio's uniqueness. There is no place in Venice for metaphor and Antonio's metaphor will become actualised.

We hear much of Portia before her entrance on the stage. Just as she steals the play she begins to steal Bassanio's attention away from Antonio. Bassanio lists her attributes in order of importance. She is first rich, then fair, and only last virtuous.

He describes her fortune to Antonio, who cares nothing of money, and we are left wondering if Bassanio knows Antonio at all. Here Bassanio is offering that Portia, with her fortune, should take Antonio's place.

> For the four winds blow in from every coast
> Renowned suitors, and her sunny locks
> Hang on her temples like a golden fleece,
> Which makes her seat of Belmont Colchos' strand,
> And many Jasons come in quest of her. (I.i.168–172)

Thus begins the leitmotif for Bassanio: In order to gain the throne, Jason and the Argonauts must capture Portia's golden fleece. As Bassanio tells Antonio of Portia we glimpse the cause of Antonio's depression. As Freud described in "Mourning and melancholia" (Freud, 1917e, pp. 243–258), with the loss of the object, in this case Bassanio, symptoms of mourning appear. Freud distinguishes mourning from depression. In mourning alone one must withdraw one's cathexis from the lost object, but in some cases this fails and one's harsh superego turns upon itself. It becomes melancholia and the self-abasement of the symptoms may be severe, and the need to expiate them can be extreme to the point of turning to masochism for relief.

Belmont is an imaginary place; ideal, rich in music and festivities. It is an imagined state like the Forest of Arden in *As You Like It* or the woods in *A Midsummer Night's Dream*, where magical events take place with the metaphor of entering nature and entering the true nature of man with fantasy and transformations. Shakespeare traditionally uses nature as a place where love objects can be interchangeable, where the distinction between classes disappears and Bottom, the jackass, can become a lover of the Queen. Here the mythical land of Belmont is also a land of dreams, and suggests possibilities for a new order. It is difficult to make a static dichotomy as to which place represents truth and which represents fantasy. Perhaps, unlike Shakespeare's other works, Belmont represents true external reality, and Venice, instead, represents internal fantasy. If this holds, then, the audience begins in fantasy, travels with the players to reality, and are returned, in the end, not to reality but to fantasy.

Portia introduces herself much like Antonio introduces himself—with a description of her melancholy. Although both have opulent wealth, it is harder for us to empathise with Portia as she says to her maid Nerissa:

> By my troth, Nerissa, my little body is aweary of
> this great world. (I.ii.1–2)

We expect her to sound powerful, but her first line is more intimate. We feel, however, her affect is a shallow impersonation of Antonio's. She is using her words to describe a feeling state like Antonio's but her jovial affect is at odds with this. She is unlike Bassanio's idealised description. She is hardly naive as he describes her, and she quickly illustrates her cleverness. She uses the language of the legal system: instructions, laws, decrees, council and reasoning. Each line foreshadows her disguise as Balthazar:

> ... I can easier teach
> twenty what were good to be done, than be one of the
> twenty to follow mine own teaching: the brain may
> devise laws for the blood, but a hot temper leaps
> o'er a cold decree,—such a hare is madness the
> youth, to skip o'er the meshes of good counsel the
> cripple; but this reasoning is not in the fashion to
> choose me a husband. (I.ii.14–21)

Portia explains that she will teach a man how to be a husband. She will not be taught how to be a wife. Still she complains of her passivity. She cannot be both powerful over her fate and obedient to her father, yet she is more obedient than she would like to be. Just as she is hardly as depressed as her words suggest, she is not so passive, even in a world where power is wielded by men. Portia knows her own heart. At this point Belmont is fantasy and affect feels false here.

Portia then goes on to satirise her suitors and we hear both her sharp wit and her cruelty. Her "melancholy" has abated.

Unlike Shakespeare's other heroines, Portia's father is dead. His presence in the play exists as the love test he had put in place to screen her suitors. He devised three caskets: one of gold, one of silver, and one of lead. The suitor who chooses wisely will find her portrait. The first, of gold, bears the inscription: "'Who chooseth me shall gain what many men desire'" (II.vii.5). The second, of silver, carries the message: "'Who chooseth me shall get as much as he deserves'" (II.vii.7). And the third, of lead, warns: "'Who chooseth me must give and hazard all he hath'" (II.vii.9). If the suitor chooses wrongly he must leave and never woo Portia again. Additionally, he himself must agree never to wed. There is a parallel with Shylock, who does not disguise himself. He says plainly of his daughter Jessica:

> I would my daughter
> were dead at my foot, and the jewels in her ear!
> would she were hears'd at my foot, and the ducats in
> her coffin. (III.i.80–83)

Thus we have another father speaking of a casket of gold. Freud was intrigued with the theme of the three caskets and concluded that this was a reappearance of the ancient Greek myth of the three Fates: Clotho, the spinner; Lachesis, the allotter; and Atropos, the inevitable, who spin, pull, and finally cut the thread of life (Freud, 1913f, pp. 291–301). The myth represents the unknowability of life's duration and the suddenness of death.

In order to raise 3,000 ducats to try his hand at the riddle of the caskets, Bassanio must borrow from Antonio. As Antonio's money is all in sea ventures he must in turn borrow from Shylock. Usury was forbidden by the Roman Catholic Church and the usurer was considered an agent of Satan, despite the many loans taken by the Church itself. Shylock explains that he wants no interest on this loan and instead proposes a metaphoric payment:

> ... let the forfeit
> Be nominated for an equal pound
> Of your fair flesh, to be cut off and taken
> In what part of your body pleaseth me. (I.iii.144–147)

This does not frighten Antonio because he is already depressed and thus a willing sacrifice for Bassanio's intended pleasure.

Some critics have suggested that Antonio's masochism is a part of his latent unconscious homosexuality. If we read the relationship as father and son, or godson, as the original source suggests, then Antonio, by making it too easy to be overcome, has increased Bassanio's problems. If Antonio gives up, then the victory is a pyrrhic victory based upon the father's weakness not upon the son's strength. Bassanio is quite self-centred and expects to get what he wants. This oedipal victory only increases his grandiosity and narcissism.

Antonio does not hide his melancholy nor does he hide his hatred. Shylock too, speaks plainly:

> With bated breath and whispering humbleness, Say this;
> 'Fair sir, you spit on me on Wednesday last;
> You spurn'd me such a day; another time
> You call'd me dog; and for these courtesies
> I'll lend you thus much moneys'? (I.iii.119–123)

To which Antonio replies, with more energy than we have seen in him:

> I am as like to call thee so again,
> To spit on thee again, to spurn thee too. (I.iii.125–126)

It seems that aggression for the sake of Bassanio also enlivens him. Antonio's anti-Semitic hatred organises him much as the Capulet/Montague feud makes for a social cohesion through projected hate.

In Belmont, Portia's maid reminds her of Bassanio as a potential suitor. Portia seems to feign a faint memory of one we suspect she remembers quite well.

Portia may appear modest and excessively feminine but she clearly knows who she would like to wed, and probably knows Bassanio's weaknesses. She is also sure that she will be able to cure him.

In Belmont one can be seen as one really is. For this reason, when Gratiano asks if he can accompany Bassanio, Bassanio recognises Gratiano, undisguised, will undo his own impersonation. Bassanio explains:

> Pray thee, take pain
> To allay with some cold drops of modesty
> They skipping spirit, lest through thy wild behaviour
> I be misconstrued in the place I go to,
> And lose my hopes. (II.ii.176–180)

Gratiano has a plan. He explains that he will "put on a sober habit", feigning sobriety and religiosity. Therefore he too shall accompany

Bassanio. Bassanio goes to Belmont costumed by Antonio's wealth. Thus they both go to Belmont in disguise.

As mentioned, Shakespearian comedies end in marriage. The three couples in the play include Portia and Bassanio, Nerissa and Gratiano, and Jessica and Lorenzo. Unlike Portia, who feigns passivity, Jessica seems to belong in a different play. Portia's father is already dead before the play begins. Jessica, however, needs to kill her father. She actively attempts to destroy Shylock. Like Portia, she disobeys her father and marries Lorenzo. Jessica does this in what our modern sensibilities would see as overly aggressive or even sociopathic. When written, this romance was part of the anti-Semitic "comedy," her solution to the dilemma is conversion. She says:

> But though I am a daughter to his blood,
> I am not to his manners. O Lorenzo,
> If thou keep promise, I shall end this strife,
> Become a Christian and thy loving wife. (II.iii.18–21)

Shylock is unable to disguise, unable to sublimate, and unable to revenge. He sees the terror and trouble in disguises. Shylock says:

> What, are there masques? Hear you me, Jessica:
> Lock up my doors; and when you hear the drum
> And the vile squealing of the wry-neck'd fife,
> Clamber not you up to the casements, then.
> Nor thrust your head into the public street. (II.v.27–31)

Jessica dresses herself as a torchbearer and robs her father's house. This suggests something of the need for Shakespeare's heroines to be active in obtaining their husbands. In disguise, Jessica says:

> Here, catch this casket: it is worth the pains.
> I am glad 'tis night, you do not look on me,
> For I am much ashamed of my exchange:
> But love is blind and lovers cannot see
> The pretty follies that themselves commit;
> For if they could, Cupid himself would blush
> To see me thus transformed to a boy. (II.vi.33–39)

Unlike Portia, who hints to Bassanio which casket holds the prize, Jessica literally steals her father's gold casket to give to Lorenzo. Jessica says: "… I have a father, you a daughter lost" (II.v.56). With this thievery and conversion she is no longer associated with Shylock.

Antonio's merchant ships have all failed and he must default on his bond.

Solanio says aptly of Antonio's feelings towards Bassanio "I think he only loves the world for him" (II.viii.50). Antonio chooses a weak love object in Bassanio, but this is a comedy of love and Eros is the blind child of Venus, and the need to love takes precedence.

After Jessica deserts Shylock, robs him, and pawns his dead wife's ring, it is clear to all that Antonio will be asked to pay the forfeit. After this profound attack, Shylock says:

> To bait fish withal: if it will feed nothing else,
> it will feed my revenge. He hath disgraced me, and
> hindered me half a million; laughed at my losses,
> mocked at my gains, scorned my nation, thwarted my
> bargains, cooled my friends, heated mine
> enemies; and what's his reason? I am a Jew. Hath
> not a Jew eyes? hath not a Jew hands, organs,
> dimensions, senses, affections, passions? fed with
> the same food, hurt with the same weapons, subject
> to the same diseases, healed by the same means,
> warmed and cooled by the same winter and summer, as
> a Christian is? If you prick us, do we not bleed?
> if you tickle us, do we not laugh? If you poison
> us, do we not die? And if you wrong us, shall we not
> revenge? If we are like you in the rest, we will
> resemble you in that. If a Jew wrong a Christian,
> what is his humility? Revenge. If a Christian
> wrong a Jew, what should his sufferance be by
> Christian example? Why, revenge. The villainy you
> teach me, I will execute, and it shall go hard but I
> will better the instruction. (III.i.47–67)

When Shylock hears that his daughter gave his wife's ring for a monkey we see that Jessica does not only destroy Shylock but also disavows her mother. Shylock says:

> Out upon her! Thou torturest me, Tubal: it was my
> turquoise; I had it of Leah when I was a bachelor:

> I would not have given it for a wilderness of monkeys.
> (III.i.110–112)

Jessica trades her mother's ring with reckless abandon. This foreshadows Portia's ring with which she binds Bassanio. Portia says:

> But when this ring
> Parts from this finger, then parts life from hence:
> O, then be bold to say Bassanio's dead! (III.ii.183–185)

Portia's ring is of unknown origins and of a less destructive history.

Back in Belmont, Portia asks Bassanio to stay a few days, then a few months, as she wants to teach him the right answer to the caskets. She gives no thought to her father designing the love test to screen suitors, nor that the discovery of the truth of the caskets may have meaning in itself. She will teach him to be the man she desires. The comparison of Portia to the golden fleece is here completed as she compares Bassanio to Hercules:

> The rest aloof are the Dardanian wives,
> With bleared visages, come forth to view
> The issue of the exploit. Go, Hercules!
> Live thou, I live: with much, much more dismay
> I view the fight than thou that makest the fray. (III.ii.58–62)

The suitor in *Il Pecorone* is told which is the correct casket (Fiorentino, reprinted in Brown, 1955, pp. 140–152). Here Bassanio discovers it for himself. There are, however, hints to where to find the answer:

> Tell me where is fancy bred,
> Or in the heart, or in the head? (III.ii.63–64)

Both words rhyme with lead. He perhaps does not need these verbal hints for he understands that outward appearances are misleading. He seems to be speaking of personal knowledge of his own disguise:

> So may the outward shows be least themselves:
> The world is still deceived with ornament.

> In law, what plea so taint'd and corrupt,
> But, being seasoned with a gracious voice,
> Obscures the show of evil? (III.ii.73–77)

He chooses the casket of lead, and we have no doubt that he will run through Portia's money as he did Antonio's. Bassanio exclaims: "We are the Jasons, we have won the fleece" (III.ii.240). Portia, like Antonio, will not mind. She cares more that she was competent and powerful in running her estate. She describes herself as:

> ... master of my servants,
> Queen o'er myself: and even now, but now,
> This house, these servants and this same myself
> Are yours, my lord: I give them with this ring;
> Which when you part from, lose, or give away,
> Let it presage the ruin of your love
> And be my vantage to exclaim on you. (III.ii.168–174)

Although she seems ready to turn over her power to Bassanio this is not exactly accurate. She has successfully rebelled again her father's control over her.

Antonio's letter interrupts the action of the play. Portia has a rival for her love and a dead Antonio would prove to be too much competition. Before he can attend to Antonio, Portia insists that they first marry.

Bassanio tells Portia how he pretended to be rich with Antonio's money only after he has won her hand in marriage, won her fortune, and secured his place as closest to her heart. Of Antonio, Bassanio says:

> Here is a letter, lady;
> The paper as the body of my friend,
> And every word in it a gaping wound,
> Issuing life-blood. (III.ii.261–264)

However, Antonio is prepared for his fate. For Portia, who has won Bassanio, has no plan to simply buy back Antonio. She is a woman of action, and Bassanio, a commodity. She embellishes the metaphor:

> Since you are dear bought, I will love you dear.
> But let me hear the letter of your friend. (III.ii.312–313)

With all her assurances that money is no object and that Bassanio should pay the bond she still goes to Venice. Perhaps it is Antonio's letter that stirs her rivalry, as Antonio writes:

> ... all debts are cleared between you and I, if I might but see you at my death. Notwithstanding, use your pleasure: if your love do not persuade you to come, let not my letter. (III.ii.317–320)

Portia will save Antonio not by her money but by her wit and cunning. We see hints of her duplicity when Portia and Nerissa dress as a young lawyer and his clerk and go to Venice disguised. As she leaves the world of Belmont for the world of Venice it seems Belmont is where things appear as the really are, and in Venice one's motives must be concealed.

Antonio, depressed, does little to protest his punishment. He says:

> Make no more offers, use no farther means,
> But will all brief and plain conveniency
> Let me have judgment and the Jew his will. (IV.i.81–83)

Antonio cannot be more ready for death. He continues:

> I am a tainted wether of the flock,
> Meetest for death: the weakest kind of fruit
> Drops earliest to the ground; and so let me
> You cannot better be employ'd, Bassanio,
> Than to live still and write mine epitaph. (IV.i.114–118)

Antonio is quite willing to accept his fate. Portia mistakes the location of the pound of flesh. She may want to cut Antonio's heart because this is where Bassanio's image resides, and she witnesses Antonio's love for Bassanio, as Antonio says:

> Say how I loved you, speak me fair in death;
> And, when the tale is told, bid her be judge
> Whether Bassanio had not once a love.
> Repent but you that you shall lose your friend,
> And he repents not that he pays your debt;
> For if the Jew do cut but deep enough,
> I'll pay it presently with all my heart. (IV.i.271–277)

Portia must destroy Shylock, although Antonio is her true target. It is her disavowed projected hatred that is deflected to Shylock.

Portia flatters Shylock into thinking that he is a Venetian and that Venetian laws would protect him. She offers him a pound of flesh, and then, in a legal argument, destroys that illusion.

> Therefore prepare thee to cut off the flesh.
> See thou no blood, nor cut thou less nor more
> But just a pound of flesh: if thou cut'st more
> Or less than just a pound, be it but so much
> As makes it light or heavy in the substance,
> Or the division of the twentieth part
> Of one poor scruple, nay, if the scale do turn
> But in the estimation of a hair,
> Thou diest and all they goods are confiscate. (IV.i.320–328)

And with that she takes everything away from him and shows him to be a satanic figure to be damned, thus preserving her relationship with Antonio.

Antonio goes from being bound to Shylock to being bound to Portia, a much more dangerous position. The Duke describes it:

> I am sorry that your leisure serves you not.
> Antonio, gratify this gentleman,
> For, in my mind, you are much bound to him. (IV.i.401–403)

Thus Portia fulfills her goal of severing Antonio and Bassanio by wit and disguise. In payment for this, Gratiano gives his wife's ring to disguised Nerissa. Bassanio, with some urging from Antonio, gives Portia's ring to disguised Portia. This is the only thing Antonio asks of him: to give away the token of his wife's love. Antonio says:

> My Lord Bassanio, let him have the ring:
> Let his deservings and my love withal
> Be valued against your wife's commandment. (IV.i.445–447)

Back in Belmont all is revealed and the rings are returned. The couples pair off and Antonio ends the play as he began it, alone.

In *The Merchant of Venice* the play moves from the world of Venice to the world of Belmont. In *Romeo and Juliet* the shift is not the move from

Verona to Mantua but rather the move from the public realm to the interpersonal and private intrapsychic domain.

The tragedy begins with the first of the sonnets. It is formal and precise, spoken by the chorus:

> Two households, both alike in dignity,
> In fair Verona, where we lay our scene,
> From ancient grudge break to new mutiny,
> Where civil blood makes civil hands unclean.
> From forth the fatal loins of these two foes
> A pair of star-cross'd lovers take their life;
> Whole misadventured piteous overthrows
> Do with their death bury their parents' strife.
> The fearful passage of their death-mark'd love,
> And the continuance of their parents' rage,
> Which, but their children's end, nought could remove,
> Is now the two hours' traffic of our stage;
> The which if you with patient ears attend,
> What here shall miss our toil shall strive to mend. (Prologue)

The source of the feud is never explained. It seems to be an immutable fact. The split feels so ancient that its origins are lost and all that remains is the taboo. The sonnet repeats this myth of which the audience was already aware.

Our introduction is to the aggressive nature of Verona's streets, which teem with heated brawls and bawdy references. Sampson says:

> Tis all one, I will show myself a tyrant: when I
> have fought with men, I will be cruel with the
> maids, and cut off their heads. (I.i.20–22)

Here a Capulet is responding to a Montague, and Romeo, in his way, will fulfil this prophecy by taking the maidenhead of a Capulet, Juliet.

Our introduction to Lord Capulet illustrates his rashness as he rushes into the streets in his dressing gown. He is ready to fight and says: "What noise is this? Give me my long sword, ho!" (I.i.73). This will prove a family trait that we see also in "fiery" (I.i.107) Tybalt and in "Ladybird" Juliet (I.iii.4). The fiery tempers on the streets are quieted when we hear Romeo's name and its associations with nature, dawn, and dew. Romeo's melancholy is described by his father before we meet him:

> Many a morning hath he there been seen,
> With tears augmenting the fresh morning dew.
> Adding to clouds more clouds with his deep sighs;
> But all so soon as the all-cheering sun
> Should in the furthest east begin to draw
> The shady curtains from Aurora's bed,
> Away from the light steals home my heavy son,
> And private in his chamber pens himself,
> Shuts up his windows, locks fair daylight out
> And makes himself an artificial night … (I.i.129–138)

Montague is concerned about his son's unhappiness and understands that he keeps his feelings to himself. He does not pretend to understand what Romeo suffers from. This is in sharp contrast with the Capulets and their relation with Juliet.

Romeo's father describes him as if he is a young, depressed Hamlet. Here the language of the play moves, as the content shifts, from public rhyme to private blank verse. Romeo is already in love with a Capulet before he even meets Juliet.

Romeo loves Rosaline. He lapses in rhyme as the only way to publicly convey love. Benvolio says:

> Alas, that love, so gentle in his view,
> Should be so tyrannous and rough in proof. (I.i.169–170)

In love with Rosaline, Romeo views love as tyrannical; in love with Juliet, he will see the world as tyrannical. While there is fighting on the streets, Romeo takes no notice. For Romeo love or the ideal of love is essential. When he speaks of love, he must speak in rhyme, but it is stereotypical and flat:

> Why, then, O brawling love! O loving hate!
> O any thing, of nothing first create!
> O heavy lightness! Serious vanity!
> Mis-shapen chaos of well-seeming forms!
> Feather of lead, bright smoke, cold fire,
> Sick health! (I.i.167–172)

Romeo will not share his feelings with Benvolio's sonnet-like sestet, which keeps inviting him to join in. Benvolio carefully rhymes a cure for love but Romeo will not rhyme back. His love is private. Romeo explains that he would feel worse if he shared his feelings: "… Which thou wilt propagate to have it prest …" (I.i.193). Romeo relies on Cupid, who cannot hit Rosaline with his arrow: "From love's weak childish bow she lives uncharm'd" (I.i.209). This begins Romeo's military imagery of courtship. We enter the Capulet's home and hear Juliet's father speak in courtly phrases about Juliet, ending in a couplet:

> And too soon marr'd are those so early made.
> The earth hath swallow'd all my hopes but she,
> She is the hopeful lady of my earth:
> But woo her, gentle Paris, get her heart,
> My will to her consent is but a part … (I.ii.13–17)

Capulet understands Juliet enough on some level to know that if Paris hopes to woo her he must first win her favour. He understands that he can't insist that she accept a husband of his choosing. This is very different than Portia's father, who controls her match even after his death.

The theme of night and day, stars, sun and moon run through this play. It begins with Romeo's depressive "artificial night," then picked up by Capulet who says:

> At my poor house look to behold this night
> Earth-treading stars that make dark heaven light. (I.ii.24–25)

Just as Montague recognises Romeo's sadness but not its cause, so too do those in Juliet's life know nothing of her internal world. Juliet's Nurse is to Juliet as Nerissa is to Portia, yet Nurse should know Juliet better because she raised her. For instance, she describes what she did to wean Juliet, but has no sense of the effect this sudden withdrawal had upon her.

> But as I said,
> When it did taste the wormwood on the nipple
> Of my dug and felt it bitter, pretty fool,
> To see it tetchy and fall out with the dug. (I.iii.29–32)

It would appear that Juliet had to retreat into an internal world because she had no sense the external world was capable of caring for her, or capable of soothing her. Even the Nurse refers to Juliet as "it." Purity of affect and not innocence is Juliet's true hallmark.

Mercutio is a confidant of Romeo. He is Antonio to Romeo's Bassanio. Mercutio prescribes the remedy for Romeo's neurasthenia, namely to find willing women and discharge his sexual tension. Mercutio is direct, bawdy, and vividly illustrative of sexuality. Romeo says:

> Is love a tender thing? It is too rough,
> Too rude, too boisterous, and it pricks like thorn. (I.iv.25–26)

To which Mercutio replies:

> If love be rough with you, be rough with love;
> Prick love for pricking, and you beat love down. (I.iv.27–28)

Mercutio's charismatic one-line rhymes to Romeo's last word forms a series of couplets between the two men. Romeo says: "I dream'd a dream to-night" (I.iv.49). To which Mercutio responds: "And so did I" (I.iv.50). Romeo asks: "Well, what was yours?" (I.iv.51). To which Mercutio responds: "That dreamers often lie" (II.iv.52). Romeo says: "In bed asleep, while they do dream things true" (I.iv.53). Mercutio ends with a couplet: "O, then, I see Queen Mab hath been with you" (I.iv.54). This demonstrates the level of intimacy between the two men, initiated by Mercutio. Soon we shall hear a more intimate version as they finish each other's lines.

Mercutio then launches into a chaotic interpretation of dreams. Queen Mab is the creator of dreams of love:

> Her chariot is an empty hazel-nut
> Made by the joiner squirrel or old grub,
> Time out o'mind the fairies' coachmakers.And in this state she gallops night by night
> Through lovers' brains, and then they dream of love. (I.iv. 59–63)

The content of Romeo's dream remains undisclosed. Mercutio says:

> True, I talk of dreams,
> Which are the children of an idle brain,
> Begot of nothing but vain fantasy,

> Which is as thin of substance as the air
> And more inconstant than the wind ... (I.iv.97–101)

One has the sense that Mercutio is not simply trying to talk Romeo out of his "humour" but rather offering himself as competition with Rosaline. The close bonding of Romeo and Mercutio takes on an anti-feminine and homosexual tenor. They are latency period boys, fearful and depreciating of women. But while Mercutio seems stuck in his development, Romeo has moved ahead albeit to idealisation.

The play takes place during December and July simultaneously, and the original source, which covered three or four months, is here condensed to three or four days. When Romeo first sees Juliet, the metaphor of birds return in rhyming couplets:

> Like a rich jewel in an Ethiope's ear;
> Beauty too rich for use, for earth too dear!
> So shows a snowy dove trooping with crows,
> As yonder lady o'er her fellows shows. (I.v.45–48)

Mercutio's cure has worked too well. By going to the Capulet party, Romeo exchanges Rosaline for Juliet.

It is the headstrong Capulet who warns Tybalt to be moderate and not fight with Romeo at the feast. In calm, private, blank verse:

> And, to say truth, Verona brags of him
> To be a virtuous and well govern'd youth;
> I would not for the wealth of all the town
> Here in my house do him disparagement:
> Therefore be patient, take no note of him ... (I.v.66–70)

This sentiment represents the law of hospitality. A guest must not be attacked in one's home even though he is the enemy. If Tybalt assaults Romeo in the Capulets' home, the play would turn into *Macbeth*.

Romeo and Juliet's first conversation is a shared sonnet in which each finishes the other's lines. Beginning as a more timid and uncertain version of the shared lines of Mercutio and Romeo, Romeo here says:

> If I profane with my unworthiest hand
> This holy shrine, the gentle fine is this:

> My lips, two blushing pilgrims, ready stand
> To smooth that rough touch with a tender kiss. (I.v.92–95)

To which Juliet responds:

> Good pilgrim, you do wrong your hand too much,
> Which mannerly devotion shows in this;
> For saints have hands that pilgrims' hands do touch,
> And palm to palm is holy palmers' kiss. (I.v.96–99)

To which Romeo answers with just one line: "Have not saints lips, and holy palmers too?" (I.v.100). Juliet answers quickly: "Ay, pilgrim, lips that they must use in prayer" (I.v.101). Romeo responds slowly with two lines:

> O, then, dear saint, let lips do what hands do;
> They pray, grant thou, lest faith turn to despair. (I.v.102–103)

Juliet rushes him onward: "Saints do not move, though grant for prayers sake" (I.v.104). Romeo finishes the sonnet: "Then move not, while my prayer's effect I take" (I.v.105–106). The sonnet ends with their kiss and a new sonnet is begun, yet it is interrupted by the Nurse.

Juliet, when overwhelmed with affect, seems to slip into tight rhyming couplets, even in private, as an attempt to contain her feelings. When she discovers Romeo is a Montague:

> My only love sprung from my only hate!
> Too early seen unknown, and known too late!
> Prodigious birth of love it is to me,
> That I must love a loathed enemy. (I.v.137–140)

The constriction of the rhyme seems to soothe her.

Act II begins, as did the play, with a sonnet by the chorus, which is somewhat more intimate than the first:

> Now Romeo is beloved and loves again,
> Alike betwitched by the charm of looks,
> But to his foe supposed he must complain,
> And she steal love's sweet bait from fearful hooks. (Prologue)

The chorus attributes the action to Juliet, as it is she that "Steal[s] love's sweet bait." Romeo has returned to Juliet's window. Mercutio cannot tolerate it, he says:

> Romeo! humours! madman! passion! lover!
> Appear thou in the likeness of a sigh:
> Speak but one rhyme, and I am satisfied;
> Cry but 'Ay me!' pronounce but 'love' and 'dove.'(II.i.7–10)

Mercutio's loss of Romeo could be soothed by language but Romeo will not comply. He deserts Mercutio for Juliet's garden.

Now the language between Romeo and Juliet is celestial. Romeo is in fear that the two can never coexist.

In Juliet's garden both break into blank verse; the rhyming couplets of courtly love are now too confining for their affects. Juliet expounds:

> What's Montague? It is nor hand, nor foot,
> Nor arm, nor face, nor any other part
> Belonging to a man. O, be some other name!
> What's in a name? that which we call a rose
> By any other name would smell as sweet ... (I.ii.40–44)

Her metaphor for Romeo here is the feminine rose. Juliet asks Romeo to swear his love. Juliet will not tolerate anything short of all, she says:

> O, swear not by the moon, the inconstant moon,
> That monthly changes in her circled orb,
> Lest that thy love prove likewise variable. (II.ii.109–111)

She knows herself and knows true affects in both herself and others. Juliet's assertiveness appears—first by keeping him there where his discovery would mean his death, she says: "If they do see thee, they will murder thee". Here her love song takes on a powerfully destructive note as she likens Romeo to a bird:

> Like a poor prisoner in his twisted gyves,
> And with a silk thread plucks it back again,
> So loving-jealous of his liberty. (II.ii.179–181)

To which Romeo responds: "I would I were thy bird" (II.ii.182). Juliet tells him darkly:

> Sweet, so would I:
> Yet I should kill thee with much cherishing. (II.ii.182–183)

The two are sharing D. W. Winnicott's potential space (Winnicott, 1971, pp. 40–41). Romeo is able to follow Juliet into her metaphor and they are able to play together in it. Something is too close to the surface and Juliet retreats into a rhyming couplet:

> Good night, good night! Parting is such sweet sorrow,
> That I shall say good night till it be morrow. (II.ii.184–185)

Romeo, in his monologue, is unaware of her retreat, and continues in the rhyming couplets that Juliet had begun:

> Sleep dwell upon thine eyes, peace in thy breast!
> Would I were sleep and peace, so sweet to rest!
> Hence will I to my ghostly father's cell,
> His help to crave, and my dear hap to tell. (II.ii.186–189)

With this parting, Romeo rushes to Friar Laurence's cell.

The Friar is a proto-Prospero, speaking of the magical properties of plants in rhyming couplets; for Friar Laurence everything is public. The Friar chides Romeo's sudden change in affection but admits that of Romeo's love for Rosaline:

> O, she knew well
> Thy love did read by rote and could not spell. (II.iii.84–85)

This reminds us that Romeo's love of Juliet changes him, and his language reflects this. The Friar continues to speak in rhyming couplets throughout this scene, breaking only in the scene's last line. Friar Laurence says: "Wisely and slow; they stumble that run fast" (II.iii.90), yet when Romeo and Juliet return that afternoon the Friar marries them.

Meanwhile Tybalt has threatened Romeo. Mercutio, accepting that Romeo is lost to him says:

> Alas poor Romeo! He is already dead; stabbed with a
> white wench's black eye; shot through the ear with a
> love-song; the very pin of his heart cleft with the

>blind bow-boy's butt-shaft: and is he a man to
>encounter Tybalt? (II.iv.13–17)

Much like Antonio, Mercutio would give all for his friend. The brawl begins between Mercutio and Tybalt. Romeo intercedes and stands between them. Romeo's attempt to stop the fight does more to increase the rage of the two men. Through Romeo's passivity Tybalt stabs Mercutio. Romeo says: "Courage, man; the hurt cannot be much" (III.i.96). To which Mercutio responds:

>No, tis not so deep as a well, nor so wide as a
>church-door; but 'tis enough, 'twill serve: ask for
>me to-morrow, and you shall find me a grave man. I
>am peppered, I warrant, for this world. A plague o'
>both your houses! 'Zounds, a dog, a rat, a mouse, a
>cat, to scratch a man to death! a braggart, a
>rogue, a villain, that fights by the book of
>arithmetic! Why the devil came you between us? I
>was hurt under your arm. (III.i.97–105)

Mercutio recognises that it was Romeo's fault. Romeo does not understand consciously his need to rid himself of Mercutio. When Romeo realises that Mercutio is dead he blames Juliet:

>O sweet Juliet,
>Thy beauty hath made me effeminate
>And in my temper soften'd valour's steel! (III.i.115–117)

Romeo, perhaps as an attempt to destroy a disavowed part of himself, must now slay Tybalt.

To Juliet, Romeo is no longer like the stars in the night sky. She wants him to be the stars:

>Give me my Romeo; and, when he shall die,
>Take him and cut him out in little stars,
>And he will make the face of heaven so fine
>That all the world will be in love with night
>And pay no worship to the garish sun. (III.ii.21–25)

The violent imagery of Romeo being cut into pieces is easily missed by the beauty of the language. The Nurse, reporting Tybalt's murder and Romeo's banishment, confuses the message, thus again reminding us how messages can be misunderstood. Here Juliet's poetry echoes that of Romeo's love note for Rosaline; each word paired with its opposite:

> Beautiful tyrant! fiend angelical!
> Dove-feather'd raven! wolvish-ravening lamb!
> Despised substance of divinest show!
> Just opposite to what thou justly seem'st,
> A damned saint, an honourable villain! (III.ii.75–79)

Yet unlike Romeo's earlier musing, here Juliet fights with true ambivalence. Juliet recovers on the side that Romeo is all:

> … For 'tis a throne where honour may be crown'd
> Sole monarch of the universal earth. (III.ii.93–94)

When Juliet understands the full extent of what has passed she calls for her family to comfort her. She returns to rhyming couplets in an attempt to contain herself. Juliet says:

> Take up those cords: poor ropes, you are beguiled,
> Both you and I; for Romeo is exiled:
> He made you for a highway to my bed;
> But I, a maid, die maiden-widowed.
> Come, cords, come, nurse; I'll to my wedding-bed;
> And death, not Romeo, take my maidenhead! (III.ii.132–137)

There is no one who can comfort her and she quickly sends the Nurse away.

Romeo, in his banishment, is able to use poetry and metaphors but can no longer rhyme. He says of his banishment:

> There is no world without Verona walls …
> Is death mis-term'd: calling death banishment,
> Thou cutt'st my head off with a golden axe,
> And smilest upon the stroke that murders me. (III.iii.17–20)

For Juliet metaphor can no longer contain her affects. Unlike Juliet, Romeo can still be soothed with words. Friar Laurence picks up on something within Romeo and attacks his vanity. Friar Laurence says:

> Hold thy desperate hand:
> Art thou a man? Thy form cries out thou art:
> Thy tears are womanish; thy wild acts denote
> The unreasonable fury of a beast:
> Unseemly woman in a seeming man!
> Or Ill-beseeming beast in seeming both! (III.iii.107–112)

Romeo and Juliet play together with shared metaphors in their own language, of iambic pentameter. This reveals their sense of time and space. Thus their courtship begins by denying dawn and ends by denying evening. Juliet says:

> Wilt thou be gone? It is not yet near day:
> It was the nightingale, and not the lark
> That pierced the fearful hollow of thine ear;
> Nightly she sings on yon pomegranate-tree:
> Believe me, love, it was the nightingale. (III.v.1–5)

Dawn, as birth, can be disavowed but evening, as death, cannot. Romeo tries to follow her denial but is unable, as he sees the day coming:

> It was the lark, the herald of the morn,
> No nightingale: look, love, what envious streaks
> Do lace the severing clouds in yonder east:
> Night's candles are burnt out, and jocund day
> Stands tiptoe on the misty mountain tops.
> I must be gone and live, or stay and die. (III.v.6–11)

While Juliet continues to deny the inevitability of dawn, Romeo, knowing that dawn will be death, no longer disagrees:

> Come, death, and welcome! Juliet wills it so.
> How is't, my soul: Let's talk; it is not day. (III.v.24–25)

Juliet is suddenly conscious of the danger we suspect she has understood for some time:

> It is, it is: hie hence, be gone, away!
> It is the lark that sings so out of tune,
> Straining harsh discords and unpleasing sharps.
> (III.v.26–28)

As Romeo leaves through the window Juliet says: "Then, window, let day in and let life out" (III.v.41). Juliet looks after him, the last time Juliet will see Romeo alive.

Believing Juliet's tears are for her dead cousin, Capulet projects his feelings on to Juliet. Capulet begins the metaphor of the sea. He says of Juliet:

> … In one little body
> Thou counterfeit'st a bark, a sea, a wind;
> For still thy eyes, which I may call the sea,
> Do ebb and flow with tears; the bark thy body is,
> Sailing in this salt flood; the winds, thy sighs;
> Who, raging with thy tears, and they with them,
> Without a sudden calm, will overset
> Thy tempest-tossed body. (III.v.131–138)

The Capulets agree to marry Juliet to Paris in great haste. Juliet refuses. When Lady Capulet tells her husband of Juliet's response she says: "I would the fool were married to her grave!" (III.v.140). Juliet's father underestimates the similarities between himself and Juliet and their shared impulsivity. When Juliet appears to easily change her love object and says she will marry Paris, Capulet says:

> … my heart is wondrous light,
> Since this same wayward girl is so reclaim'd. (IV.ii.46–47)

In this instance he again does not recognise his daughter's inner state. Desperate not to be passive, Juliet says:

> I'll go the friar, to know his remedy:
> If all else fail, myself have power to die. (III.v.241–242)

Juliet has lost all metaphor and poetry. She says to Friar Laurence:

> Be not so long to speak; I long to die,
> If what thou speak'st speak not of remedy. (IV.i.66–67)

Juliet shows fear and hesitation before she drinks Friar Laurence's magic potion. She ponders:

> What if it be a poison, which the Friar
> Subtly hath minister'd to have me dead,
> Lest in this marriage he should be dishonour'd,
> Because he married me before to Romeo? ... (IV.iii.24–27)
> ... alack, alack, is it not like that I
> So early waking, what with loathsome smells,
> And shrieks like mandrakes torn out of the earth,
> That living mortals, hearing them, run mad ... (IV.iii.45–48)
> ... O, look! Methinks I see my cousin's ghost
> Seeking out Romeo, that did split his body
> Upon a rapier's point: stay, Tybalt, stay! (IV.iii.55–57)

Even in her most extreme desperation she has the capacity to ponder the motives of others.

Lord Capulet discovers Juliet's body and believes her dead. He says:

> ... There she lies,
> Flower as she was, deflowered by him.
> Death is my son-in-law, Death is my heir;
> My daughter he hath wedded: I will die,
> And leave him all; life, living, all is Death's. (IV.v.36–40)

Ironically, what he wished for if Juliet disobeyed him has now come to be.

Friar Laurence believes that Juliet will wake and end the strife between the families. It is in part Friar Laurence's grandiosity that leads to the play's final act.

Again speech is paired with opposites: first in Romeo's stiff poetry of "cold fire" and "feather of lead", (I.i.171) then in Juliet's struggle with her opposing affects, and finally Lord Capulet shares his ambivalence with antonyms as he says:

> Our instruments to melancholy bells,
> Our wedding cheer to a sad burial feast,
> Our solemn hymns to sullen dirges change,
> Our bridal flowers serve for a buried corse,
> And all things change them to the contrary. (IV.v.86–90)

In Mantua, Balthasar informs Romeo that Juliet is dead. Without Hamlet's hesitation, Romeo already knows what he is going to do and already knows where to find his poison.

Juliet, throughout the course of the play, turns Romeo from a boy of ideas into a man of action. Romeo says to Balthasar:

> By heaven, I will tear thee joint by joint
> And strew this hungry churchyard with thy limbs:
> The time and my intents are savage-wild,
> More fierce and more inexorable far
> Than empty tigers or the roaring sea. (V.iii.35–39)

At Juliet's tomb he encounters Paris. Romeo says: "Good gentle youth, tempt not a desperate man" (V.iii.59). When Paris will not leave, the once passive Romeo says: "Wilt thou provoke me? Then have at thee, boy!" (V.iii.70). Romeo quickly slays Paris and enters the crypt. Romeo sees Juliet in the disguise of death:

> … Ah, dear Juliet,
> Why are thou yet so fair? shall I believe
> That unsubstantial death is amorous,
> And that the lean abhorred monster keeps
> Thee here in the dark to be his paramour? (V.iii.102–106)

The metaphor of Juliet as ocean returns, and Romeo now is the ship lost in that ocean. Concluding the metaphor Capulet had begun:

> Come, bitter conduct, come, unsavoury guide!
> Thou desperate pilot, now at once run on
> The dashing rocks thy sea-sick weary bark!
> Here's to my love!
> O true apothecary!
> Thy drugs are quick. Thus with a kiss I die. (V.iii.116–121)

Juliet awakes to find Romeo dead. Juliet had been passive with Friar Laurence, allowing him to take the lead. Rather than passively poisoning herself, allowing the poison to kill her, Juliet stabs herself in an active killing.

> Yea, noise? Then I'll be brief. O happy dagger!
> This is thy sheath;
> There rust, and let me die. (V.iii.168–170)

She is active and powerful even in her death.

If order is restored in the rhythm of the language then order will be restored in Verona. The prince's rhyming couplets soothe us:

> A glooming peace this morning with it brings;
> The sun, for sorrow, will not show his head:
> Go hence, to have more talk of these sad things;
> Some shall be pardon'd, and some punished:
> For never was a story of more woe
> Than this of Juliet and her Romeo. (V.iii.304–309)

It is interesting that both *The Merchant of Venice* and *Romeo and Juliet* were written in the year 1596. They resemble Franz Alexander's concept in "Dreams in Pairs and Series" (Alexander, 1921, pp. 31–36) in which he concluded that dreams of the same night have similar motivation but different manifest content.

Both heroines must accomplish or fail to resolve the female oedipal situation. Portia is educated and elegant. Juliet is strong and determined. Both must rebel against their father's choices for husbands. Portia actively discouraged suitors that were not of her choosing. Juliet impulsively married Romeo. Both use the disguise of compliance; however, these are strong women who know their own hearts and must only appear passive in a world where power is wielded by men.

Choice, however, is only the beginning, for they will have to elicit the caring and maternal aspects of their men. Both women must remove, in some way, their men's earlier love object. Mercutio is murdered and Antonio is subjected to Portia, thus both women defeat their male rivals. Bassanio must become more of a husband and caretaker (lead casket), than simply a lover who is enamoured of Portia's wealth and status (gold casket). Romeo has to be a lover of a real woman and not simply an idealiser. Both men have to transition from idealised and idealising lovers to sexual objects.

Juliet's tragedy is that her inner world is known only to herself. Of her suitors, Paris is far the more suitable. To the feudal age, Paris is of the Capulet clan and declares in stately couplets and sonnets his idealised love for Juliet. He knows nothing of Juliet's inner life, neither do her parents or the Nurse. They all assume, on the basis of their own projections, what is in Juliet's pre-conscious. If, by chance, they learn of Juliet's true thoughts, such as "I have not thought of marriage," they disavow such feelings and substitute their own—that is, not what she thinks but what she should think. Lady Capulet's response to Juliet is: I was married and with child when I was your age. Capulet takes Juliet's refusal to marry Paris as a direct assault on his maleness and threatens to disown her if she does not obey him.

Portia forgives Bassanio's shortcomings even when he gives her ring away to herself in disguise. Juliet does not need to forgive Romeo's slaying of Tybalt. Her love is relentless and, although Romeo complains that her love has made him effeminate, it is that eliciting of the feminine part of him that permits "the marriage of true minds" (Sonnets cxvi.1). It seems the task of the woman in these two plays is to find the feminine in the male. Solutions such as these are never perfect or complete, but must be repeated and re-solved during one's lifetime.

Romeo and Juliet illustrates specific references to a society mired in feudal traditions and expresses a hope for change that echoed the sentiments of its Renaissance audience. The drama stresses the individual over the collective, and manages to appeal to contemporary life histories. Juliet is Shakespeare's Antigone, and like the Sophocles heroine, she is a strong woman who stresses the human over the arbitrary state. Antigone's death is her victory over Creon's revenge, and the King of Thebes suffers the loss of his son, just as the Montagues and Capulets lose their offspring.

The feudal society demanded clear separation of male and female lives and allowed little variance in gender roles. The separation and individuation phase in development (Mahler, 1968, pp. 221–226) was denied. Children had to be like their parents and all change had to be disavowed. What is universal in this play is that parents are the enemies of adolescents and the need to become authentic is the task for this period of life. The need to desexualise the parent of the opposite sex and de-aggressivise the parent of the same sex are conflicts that need to be resolved. This is evident for Romeo, as the male resolution of the oedipal situation seems easier than that of the female. Romeo achieves this through the love of Juliet. Women seem to have a more difficult time, for they have to change their love objects from female (mother) to male (father) and then to lover (husband).

Aristototle defines tragedy as:

> a process of imitating an action which has serious implications, is complete, and possesses magnitude; by means of language which has been made sensuously attractive, with each of its varieties found separately in the parts; enacted by the persons themselves and not presented through narrative; through a course of pity and fear completing the purification of tragic acts which have those emotional characteristics. (Aristotle, 335 BCE, p. 25)

Through *Romeo and Juliet*, Shakespeare became a true tragedian according to the Aristotelian definition. It tells a specific myth with universal meaning, and has a profound effect on the audience by permitting the discharge of emotions, which is cathartic in itself.

CHAPTER FOUR

Visions of self in *Julius Caesar*

This Roman play by William Shakespeare is referred to as his first mature tragedy and is only half the length of *Hamlet*. It was written and performed in 1599 (Platter, 1599, pp. 139–161), and is the play that Shakespeare chose to open the Globe Theatre. The plot appears simple and direct. There is little humour by contemporary or even Elizabethan standards. It is a drama dominated by men and in which its only two women are not listened to, and are both refused. There are gruesome murders and suicides performed on the stage. It is not just a play of action, as there are poetic passages and fine lines, perhaps none more famous than Antony's funeral oration. These words and phrases entered our language and remain there, such as "Et tu, Brute", "the dogs of war", and "cowards die many times, the valiant but once". There are omens, supernatural storms, dreams, and even a visitation from a ghost; shades of what was to come in both *Hamlet*, and *Macbeth*. The ending cleanly resolves the conflicts raised in the play. It is no wonder that educators use this play as an introduction to Shakespeare. When the senior author first read it in the seventh grade it seemed a "blood and guts" thriller. It was only later in life with re-reading, and seeing film and stage versions that the drama revealed its psychological depth. While *Hamlet* demands much of the audience (one must come to grips with the conflict of guilty passivity *vs.* action and revenge) this play requires less of us. Caesar, Mark Antony, Brutus, Cassius, and Cicero were real people; yet this is not a pure history play. In 1579, Sir Thomas North translated Plutarch's *Lives of Noble Grecians and Romans*. It has been shown that this book was in Shakespeare's personal library, and Shakespeare read and clearly absorbed its contents. He based three of his plays on the material he gleaned from North's translation: *Coriolanus, Antony and Cleopatra*, and *Julius Caesar*. Plutarch's names and plots also appear in other Shakespeare plays; however, unlike the others, here Shakespeare remains close to his source (Plutarch, 1579, pp. 119–213).

Many critics have questioned why it is called *Julius Caesar*, when he has but 130 lines and is killed in Act III,—roughly halfway through the drama. Brutus, by contrast, is on stage for most of the play and has six times the amount of lines. Caesar has no extensive monologues and no soliloquies, unlike Brutus, Antony, or Cassius. Why was it named Julius Caesar? Perhaps, although murdered, Caesar is still a commanding figure in the inner lives of the characters who survive him.

Caesar's heir, Octavius, became the first Roman emperor, Augustus, and used Caesar as his surname, as did the ensuing emperors for the next 500 years. The name became synonymous with the rulers of Rome. Brutus' line ended with his death, and his name is evoked to express treachery and conspiracy. Caesar himself was a great warrior who expanded the Roman state and devised the calendar, which remained in effect until 1582. Caesar's calendar moved from a natural lunar twenty-eight day calendar to one closer to the scientific calendar we currently use.

Time in the play is tightly condensed, as in a dream. Theatre, like Caesar, is an innovator of time. For Shakespeare, all time was the two and a half hours in the afternoon during which his plays were performed.

The play begins with workers dressed in their finest clothes, on their way to cheer Caesar on his return from defeating Pompey in the civil war. The plebeians joke with the two republican senators using puns, some ribald ones. The cobbler says his work is:

> A trade, sir, that I hope I may use with a safe
> conscience which is indeed, sir, a mender of bad soles.
> (I.i.13–14)

Thus the play begins with a reference to the primitive. The cobbler says something of animism; although in jest, he suggests spirits exist in all of nature. The senators complain that the fickle crowd cheered Pompey when he won a battle a year before and now cheer his defeat with equal enthusiasm.

The city is decorated and the senators are going to tear the laurels off Caesar's statues and downplay the celebration. This scene is the prelude to one of the play's themes, the capriciousness of the masses *vs.* the consistency of the high-minded. Although quite close to his source throughout the play, this conflict between the senators and the plebeians comes directly from Shakespeare.

Caesar, while neither king nor emperor, essentially acts as the chieftain of Rome and is subject to the rules of kingship as described by Sir James G. Frazer and metabolised by Sigmund Freud, who used Frazer's insights in *Totem and Taboo*. Freud describes the phenomenon:

> ... the ruler is believed to exercise great authority over the forces of Nature, but that he has to be most carefully protected against the threat of danger—as though his own power, which can do so much, cannot do this. The situation is made still more difficult by the fact that the ruler cannot be trusted to make use of his immense powers in the right way, that is, for the benefit of his subjects and for his own protection. Thus people distrust him and feel justified in keeping a watch on him. The etiquette of taboos to which the king's whole life is subjected serves all these protective purposes at once: his own protection from dangers and the protection of his subjects from the dangers with which he threatens them. (Freud, 1912–1913, p. 48)

Caesar is exalted, but only as long as he maintains the status quo among his subjects and preserves balance between his subjects and nature.

This day is also the feast of Lupercal. The young men, including Mark Antony, will run naked through the streets, dressed only in a goatskin thong. Caesar bids Antony to touch Caesar's wife Calpurnia; this metaphoric simulation of intercourse is hoped to cure her infertility. A soothsayer appears and warns Caesar: "Beware the Ides of March" (I.ii.23). The soothsayer represents the priest of an earlier period, who protects the natural order. The Ides of March is not simply a date but represents something ancient that transcends the Julian calendar. Caesar first breaks the natural order when he dismisses the soothsayer, saying: "He is a dreamer. Let us leave him" (I.ii.24). Caesar is now dangerously breaking with the ancient system.

In the next scene Brutus and Cassius are alone. Cassius, a keen observer, notes that Brutus is staying away from the festivities—a fact of significance that Brutus himself may not recognise. Brutus demurs and says he is serious: "I am not gamesome" (I.ii.28). At that moment Brutus does not recognise the struggle he has within himself concerning Caesar's victory. Brutus continues:

> I do lack some part
> Of that quick spirit that is in Antony. (I.ii.39–40)

Brutus emphasises the difference between himself and Antony. Brutus has introduced a potential schism—which is not lost on Cassius. This unconscious reaction to Antony, whether love, hate, or jealousy, is never brought to the fore, and as it is unrecognised by Brutus it will play a part in Brutus' undoing. Cassius here begins his seduction of Brutus, chiding him for being unfriendly. Cassius says:

> I have not from your eyes that gentleness
> And show of love as I was wont to have. (I.ii.33–34)

Cassius uses the word "love" frequently, not to express affect, but to emphasise to Brutus how similar they are, or how similar Cassius wishes Brutus to believe them to be.

Cassius, like a psychoanalyst, recognises the ambivalence with which Brutus struggles. While ambivalence in itself is a naturally occurring phenomenon of simultaneous experience of opposite affects, under stress or the strength of these feelings one of the two affects reaches consciousness while the other remains repressed, out of awareness (Freud, 1905d, pp. 135–243). For his own reasons, he wants Brutus to identify his negative feelings towards Caesar. Brutus says:

> Be not deceived. If I have veiled my look,
> I turn the trouble of my countenance
> Merely upon myself. Vexed I am
> Of late with passions of some difference,
> Conceptions only proper to myself
> Which give some soil, perhaps to my behaviours. (I.ii.37–42)

This is unlike the analytic situation, as it is Cassius who comes to Brutus. Brutus does not seek Cassius to unburden himself. Brutus says only that he has turned inward, but requests no relief.

Cassius wants to use Brutus as a figurehead for his rebellion. Brutus is unaware that Caesar awarding him a political seat that Cassius was clearly more suited to may affect Cassius' feelings. Cassius has already gotten Brutus to admit aloud more than he intended, and now, as Brutus attempts to seal off these feelings, Cassius draws Brutus back with flattery, playing off Brutus' disavowed grandiosity: "the maintenance of even the diseased remnant of the self is preferable to not being, that is, to accept the take over of another's personality" (Kohut, 1984, p. 142). Cassius does this with an Iago-like cleverness. He uses the image of a mirror in which others see Brutus more exalted than he sees himself. Cassius explains:

> ... the eye does not see itself
> But by reflection of a mirror (I.ii.52–53)

This is the psychological insight into the preconsciousness of the ego or the self. Here, Cassius suggests that Brutus can only be enlivened by the reflection of another, as in Heinz Kohut's (Kohut, 1984, pp. 183–184) mirror transference. However, unlike Kohut's understanding of the psychoanalytic process in which the development of a mirroring transference is intended to facilitate growth, mirroring in this context has a manipulative intention. What Brutus is undergoing may be described as D. W. Winnicott's "False Self", when the false self prevents and inhibits what Winnicott describes as the "spontaneous gesture" of the true self. This compromise comes at a great cost to the individual (Winnicott, cited by Jacobus, 2005, p. 160). Cassius says:

> That you have no such mirrors as will turn
> Your hidden worthiness into your eye,
> That you might see your shadow. (I.ii.56–58)

Brutus is lulled in and Cassius continues:

> Where many of the best respect in Rome
> (Except immortal Caesar) speaking of Brutus,
> And groaning underneath this age's yoke,
> Have wished that noble Brutus had his eyes. (I.ii.59–62)

The same is not true for Cassius. Brutus responds much like a patient faced with a premature interpretation; despite the potential accuracy of the interpretation, the individual walls himself off through the defences of resistance and projection.

Brutus, too, responds with resistance. Brutus, clearly stirred, disavows his feelings while using Cassius as an example of the "mirror transference". This phenomenon describes the transfer of early or archaic narcissistic needs for empathic attunement, recognition and validation onto the analyst or essential others in the person's life. The essential other who responds optimally to these needs serves a selfobject function, in which they are experienced by the person as a part of his or her self-system (Kohut, 1971, pp. xiv–34).

> Into what dangers would you lead me, Cassius,
> Than you would have me seek into myself
> For that which is not in me? (I.ii.64–66)

When one projects unconscious feelings onto another individual, this act protects one's own consciousness from "knowing". The individual must organise one's psyche into a cohesive configuration, and establish self-sustaining relationships between oneself and the external world. Anna Freud wrote: "… we can already speak with greater certainty about the parallels between the ego's defensive measures against external and internal danger" (Freud, 1936, p. 190). Brutus while seeming involved in this discussion is hypervigilant, observing all that occurs around him. When noises are heard off stage, Brutus reacts. Brutus puts his feelings into words as he says:

> What means this shouting? I do fear the people
> Choose Caesar for their King. (I.ii.78–79)

Cassius hears Brutus' disapproval and says:

> Ay, do you fear it?
> Then must I think you would not have it so. (I.ii.80–81)

Brutus responds, "I would not, Cassius, yet I love him well." (I.ii.82) Here we observe the positive side of his ambivalence towards Caesar. Then suddenly he shuts down, saying:

> But wherefore do you hold me here so long?
> What is it that you would impart to me? (I.ii.83–84)

He is now angry with Cassius for getting him to reveal these inner feelings. Brutus continues:

> For let the gods so speed me as I love
> The name of honour more than I fear death. (I.ii.88–89)

Cassius' flattery acts as an introject: "I know that virtue to be in you, Brutus" (I.ii.90). The more Brutus is called virtuous the more virtuous he believes himself to be. Introjects are what one takes from the external world, and become part of one's internal structure. They can then be subject to defence mechanisms such as denial, projection, and disavowal. In connection with this point, Christopher Bollas describes an interactional process in which the person introjects the object's way of managing or interacting with him, which can result in an intrapsychic experience of his self as objectified by the other (Bollas, 1987, pp. 13–170). Each moment that Brutus reveals a vulnerability, Cassius utilises it. Cassius follows the negative side of Brutus' ambivalence by telling two stories to denigrate Caesar's superhuman qualities and his masculinity. Cassius begins by recounting a dare that Caesar once put to him:

> For once upon a raw and gusty day,
> The troubled Tiber chafing with her shores,
> Caesar says to me, 'Dar'st thou, Cassius, now
> Leap in with me into this angry flood
> And swim to yonder point? ... (I.ii.100–104)
>
> ... But ere we could arrive the point proposed
> Caesar cried: 'Help me Cassius, or I sink!' (I.ii.110–111)

Cassius then describes Caesar in Spain:

> Alas it cried, 'give me some drink, Titinius',
> As a sick girl. (I.ii.127–128)

He refers to Caesar first as a girl and then as "it". As Cassius is subtly dehumanising Caesar, Brutus again is stirred in a paranoid reaction, misperceiving, with a hypervigilance, to these slights. The stirring of vengeful feelings in these reactions are relatively common. Once again he hears the roaring of the crowds, and imagines new honours bestowed on Caesar.

Brutus' feelings towards Caesar are complicated. The Elizabethan audience knew from Plutarch that Caesar had a sexual relationship with Brutus' mother, Servilia. Caesar himself fantasised that he was Brutus' father (Plutarch, 1579, p. 247). It is interesting that Shakespeare does not reveal this relationship in the play; instead he disguises it as a father-son-like relationship, but, however disguised, it is ridden with the same conflict and motivation as if it were a true father–son relationship. It is more difficult to understand Cassius' motivations. He desires not only to overthrow the government, but also to destroy Caesar. From the perspective of psychoanalytic self-psychology, the rupture of an experienced merger with an omnipotent selfobject can be felt as an assault on the self and result in narcissistic rage, often directed at the total destruction of the selfobject. Perhaps, through Cassius' eyes, Caesar's frailty results in the de-idealisation of a paternal figure, and this motivates him. Indeed, Cassius shifts quickly to describe Caesar as if a giant:

> Like a Colossus, and we petty men
> Walk under his huge legs and peep about
> To find ourselves dishonourable graves. (I.ii.135–137)

Caesar, then, appears as in a son's view of his all-powerful father. If Caesar is Colossus, Cassius must be diminished. He continues:

> Men at some time are masters of their fates.
> The fault, dear Brutus, is not in our stars
> But in ourselves. (I.ii.139–141)

Cassius sounds as if he is speaking about self-will; yet this line is often quoted without its conclusion: "… That we are underlings" (I.ii.141). Cassius is not talking about self-determination, but rather is externalising blame. Cassius recognises Brutus' passivity and uses these lines to encourage Brutus to act. He reminds Brutus that he has a long family history of resisting tyrants. Brutus acknowledges that he has had such thoughts, but does not want to be pushed by Cassius any further.

The closeness and intimacy of this exchange seem to drown out all else—even Rome itself.

> That you do love me, I am nothing jealous:
> What you would work me to, I have some aim:
> How I have thought of this and of these times
> I shall recount hereafter. (I.ii.161–164)

Brutus expression, "I am nothing jealous" is fitting, as jealousy is an unspoken leitmotif of the drama. Although the first recorded use of "jealousy" precedes this play by two hundred years, it is often believed to be one of the first recorded uses of the word in the English language.

As Caesar and the rest of Rome return we observe Brutus' hypervigilance. He has the ability to observe subtle affect in others. He describes what he sees:

> The angry spot doth glow on Caesar's brow,
> And all the rest look like a chidden train:
> Calpurnia's cheek is pale, and Cicero
> Looks with such ferret and such fiery eyes … (I.ii.182–185)

It is as if Brutus feels that all his thoughts and feelings are public—he needs to tune into others to ensure his safety. Brutus has the ability to read their emotions from their faces.

We are introduced to the relationship between Caesar and Antony, as Caesar confides:

> Yond Cassius has a lean and hungry look:
> He thinks too much: such men are dangerous. (I.ii.192–193)

Antony misunderstands Caesar. He tries to reassure Caesar not to be fearful of Cassius. Caesar is being paternal. He explains that men like Cassius, who derive little pleasure from life, are usually envious plotters. He tells Antony:

> Come on my right hand, for this ear is deaf,
> And tell me truly what thou think'st of him. (I.ii.212–213)

While we define tragic figures as those who cannot recognise their flaws, unlike other tragic figures Caesar can recognise his physical failings and losses and even talks freely about his infirmities. He is an early King Lear, who fears he is not in his "perfect mind" (IV.vii.63) but Shakespeare is not ready to deal with an aging man. Lear is eighty as his play begins, Caesar fifty-five, and Shakespeare only thirty-five when he wrote *Julius Caesar*.

Brutus, always listening to all around him, questions Caska about the noises he heard during the race; it is as Brutus has suspected. Caska adds another dimension to the conspiracy. It is clear he is on the side of Cassius, as he describes the mock crowning of Caesar in raw, blunt prose. He sounds very different from the "high ideals" of Brutus. Caska is the bandit, and he wants revolution, with no need of a higher purpose. He hypothesises that Caesar creates psychogenic epilepsy to play on the crowd's sympathy for his human frailty. Using one of the few bawdy puns in the play, Caska says that if Caesar "stabbed" (i.e., had intercourse) with their mothers, they would have "done no less". In these lines Shakespeare seems to suggest that all women belong to Caesar. Shakespeare is touching upon the concept of the primal horde put forth by Charles Darwin and elaborated on by Freud in *Totem and Taboo*, and later in *Moses and Monotheism*, which describes how in prehistory all women belong to the father and from this arises the hatred of the band of sons. In Freud's view, this serves as the precursor of the Oedipus complex, which is forever repeated in fantasy in the course of normal human development: "the boy's sexual wishes in regard to his mother become more intense and his father is perceived as an obstacle to them" (Freud, 1923b, p. 32). When Cassius asks Caska what the poet said, Caska replies:

> those that understood him, smiled at one
> Another and shook their heads; but for
> Mine own part, it was Greek to me. (I.ii.281–283)

Caska, like Cassius, does not enjoy the arts. Brutus does not think much of Caska and says of him:

> What a blunt fellow is this grown to be!
> He was quick mettle when he went to school. (I.ii.294–295)

VISIONS OF SELF IN *JULIUS CAESAR* 93

Cassius, having an understanding of the full plot explains to Brutus that it is better to be open and coarse than to be thoughtful and inactive:

> This rudeness is a sauce to his good wit,
> Which gives men stomach to digest his words
> With better appetite. (I.ii.299–301)

As a precursor to Hamlet, Cassius says, essentially, action will set you free. Brutus and Cassius arrange to meet, and we see their closeness, as Brutus says:

> I will come home to you: or, if you will,
> Come home to me, and I will wait for you. (I.ii.304–305)

By emphasising the public and private worlds, both physically and linguistically, we understand that Cassius has now entered Brutus' private world and has access to his inner self. Cassius parts, enticing Brutus: "Till then, think of the world" (I.ii.306). Thus he is again stirring Brutus' grandiosity.

Seduction to Cassius is alchemic. Instead of changing lead to gold he desires to change gold into lead; Brutus' virtue into baser traits. Alone, Cassius says of Brutus:

> Thy honourable metal may be wrought
> From that it is disposed. Therefore it is meet
> That noble minds keep ever with
> Their likes; for who so firm that cannot be seduced?
> (I.ii.308–311)

It then seems almost too simple that Cassius' next move is to forge notes to throw into Brutus' window "as if they came from several citizens …" (I.ii.316). Perhaps, recognising Brutus' walled-off paranoia, grandiosity, and isolation, this is exactly the tactic to take, easily making Cassius' singular suggestion appear to come from many. Thus as sloppy a plan as this may appear, it is exactly the plan Brutus would respond to.

The next scene is announced by thunder and lightning. While not Shakespeare's first use of these stage effects they were new and modern to the audience of the Globe. When Caska meets Cicero during the great storm he is terrified.

> ... I have seen
> The ambitious ocean swell, and rage, and foam,
> To be exalted with the threatening clouds:
> But never till tonight, never till now,
> Did I go through a tempest dropping fire.
> Either there is a civil strife in heaven,
> Or else the world, too saucy with the gods,
> Incenses them to send destruction. (I.iii.6–13)

To which rational Cicero, without plots and schemes on his mind, responds: "Why, saw you any thing more wonderful?" (I.iii.15). Cicero elaborates the concept of projection: each sees himself in the storm. Caska, shaken, continues:

> And yesterday the bird of night did sit
> Even at noonday upon the market-place
> Hooting and shrieking. (I.iii.26–28)

The storm has switched Caska's prose to verse. Cicero explains:

> Indeed it is a strange-disposed time.
> But men may construe things after their fashion
> Clean from the purpose of the things themselves. (I.iii.33–35)

Cassius does not believe in the gods, and we see an extension of this, as he cannot idealise Caesar either. Cassius views the storm as a naturally occurring event. This does not stop him, however, from using it to his advantage. Caska asks fearfully: "Whoever knew the heavens menace so?" (I.iii.44). Cassius, again assuming an all—knowing position, responds: "Those that have known the earth so full of faults" (I.iii.45). Cassius then makes a great show of his bravery:

> I have walk'd about the streets ...
> Have bared my bosom to the thunder-stone:
> And when the cross blue lightening seemed to open
> The breast of heaven, I did present myself
> Even in the aim and very flash of it. (I.iii.46–50)

Cassius is consciously aware of his own aggression; therefore, the storm cannot frighten him.

> I know where I will wear this dagger then:
> Cassius from bondage will deliver Cassius. (I.iii.89–90)

Caska picks up on Cassius' alchemy metaphor and says of Brutus:

> O he sits high in all the peoples' hearts:
> And that which would appear offence in us
> His countenance, like richest alchemy,
> Will change to virtue and to worthiness. (I.iii.157–160)

Instead of attempting to diminish Brutus, as Cassius does, Caska says their lead plan will become gold if Brutus joins them. Brutus, like Cassius, believes that the storm is an act of nature and takes no notice of it. He says to Lucius, his servant:

> I cannot by the progress of the stars
> Give guess how near to day. (II.i.2–3)

With this statement, we feel Brutus' distraction. We are reminded of the importance of time, and the changes Caesar made to the calendar. It also represents our countdown to Caesar's murder.

With jealousy and ambition, Brutus' monologue begins with his conclusion that he must murder Caesar. Although Brutus is not entirely convinced at the beginning of his soliloquy, he allows himself to follow his words and ultimately convinces himself, concluding with a rationalisation of his decision. He says:

> But 'tis a common proof
> That lowliness is young ambition's ladder
> Where to the climber upward turns his face;
> But when he once attains the upmost round
> He then unto the ladder turns his back,
> Looks in the clouds, scorning the base degrees
> By which he did ascend. So Caesar may. (II.i.21–27)

Brutus now strongly answers the question he began so timidly:

> And therefore think him as a serpent's egg
> Which hatched, would as his kind grow mischievous,
> And kill him in the shell. (II.i.32–34)

This soothing, hypnotic speech, like a subtle slither of its serpent, occurs during, and contrasts with, the great storm. Brutus is not moved by the storm—or perhaps the storm is created by him, a metaphor and projection for his inner conflicts. Again time collapses and rushes on. Brutus asks: "Is not tomorrow, boy, the Ides of March?" (II.i.40). Lucius' sleepiness emphasises Brutus' insomnia. This sleeplessness may be our first sign of the fragmentation of his self-system and descent into madness.

> Since Cassius first did whet me against Caesar
> I have not slept. (II.i.61–62)

Since Cassius awoke what was "sleeping" inside Brutus, Brutus has not slept. As the conspirators increase in number and meet in the night, Brutus comments on the darkness of the plan.

> O conspiracy,
> Sham'st thou to show thy dangerous brow by night,
> When evils are most free? O then by day
> Where wilt thou find a cavern dark enough
> To mask thy monstrous visage? (II.i.77–81)

Brutus clings to his "noble" motives more desperately. While seeming to feel some remorse he still splits off his affects, objectifying the group and referring to it as a conspiracy, rather than personifying it as a collection of conspirators; thus he is not yet embracing his role in it. When Cassius asks all to swear their "resolution" Brutus publicly opposes Cassius. Brutus says:

> "No, not an oath ..." (II.i.102)

and continues:

> ... do not stain
> The even virtue of our enterprise. (II.i.131–132)

Cassius interrupts Brutus—asking Cicero to join—which derails Brutus' speech. Each conspirator then interjects their view of Cicero, drowning out Brutus' words. This subtle shift creates the sense of inevitability of the plot. Brutus now disagrees with Cassius a second time, and each disagreement strengthens his overt resolve. The more Cassius snubs him, the more resolved Brutus is to murder Caesar and believes it is his own idea, his own "serpent's egg". Brutus, hyper in tune to others, says:

> O name him not. Let us not break with him,
> For he will never follow anything
> That other men begin. (II.i.149–151)

Interrupted and derailed, Brutus has come to believe from Cassius that he himself is special and required by Rome to murder Caesar. As Cassius interrupts him, Brutus' grandiosity grows. Cassius says: "Let Antony and Caesar fall together" (II.i.160). Cassius overestimates what Brutus has become.

Brutus, clinging to altruistic rationalisations, responds: "Our course will seem too bloody, Caius Cassius …" (II.i.161). Here resorting to his formal name and claiming ownership of the plan, Brutus continues:

> … To cut the head off and then hack the limbs—
> like wrath in death and envy afterwards … (II.i.162–163)

Much like the plague on Thebes, so, too, Rome seems to suffer a plague that requires a sacrifice to appease the gods, although neither Brutus nor Cassius believe in the gods. Brutus talks about the murder as if it will be a surgical excision and not butchery. The problem will be that, when he "surgically removes" Caesar, Brutus will destroy himself; Caesar is not only an external object, but also an internal object—a part of him. Brutus says: "Let us be sacrificers but not butchers, Caius" (II.i.165). Brutus continues:

> Let's kill him boldly, but not wrathfully:
> Let's carve him as a dish fit for the gods,
> Not hew him as a carcass fit for hounds. (II.i.171–173)

Brutus still does not understand the true ramifications of the plan for Rome nor for himself. He says: "We shall be called purgers, not murderers" (II.i.179), and he reasons that therefore it is not a murder. A conspirator is then interrupted by the clock striking—reminding us again of the brisk passage of time. Decius acts as a self-appointed clown, bragging of his ability to distract and manipulate Caesar:

> I can o'ersway him: for he loves to hear
> That unicorns may be betrayed with trees,
> And bears with glasses, elephants with holes
> Lions with toils and men with flatterers.
> But when I tell him he hates flatterers,
> He says he does, being then most flattered. (II.i.202–207)

He finishes, using the strong monosyllables for which the play is well known. Decius, like Scheherazade in *The Arabian Nights*, uses the tactic of keeping Caesar amused with tales of exotic imagery. Previously, he used this tactic to avoid his own destruction, now he will use it to lead Caesar to his death.

Brutus continues the countdown: "By the eighth hour …" (II.i.212). Cassius and Brutus begin to dance with language, not unlike Romeo and Juliet. Each sentence is answered by the other—Brutus attempts to restrain the conspirators and Cassius to excite them.

Brutus and Caesar are the only two characters whose wives are named and who appear in the drama. Portia, Brutus' wife complains that he has been distant from her. She wonders if she has done something to offend him. She thinks it might be a choleric mood, yet when it does not pass, as such humours usually do, she realises that something else is troubling him. She wants to share his thoughts because they married in love. She explains to him that she is not a harlot who shares his bed but a Roman lady of good family, being Cato's daughter.

> I have made strong proof of my constancy,
> Giving myself a voluntary wound,
> Here in the thigh. (II.i.298–300)

This wound to the thigh is a metaphor for self-castration and suggests she gave up her maleness and power to be his wife. Brutus seems to be moved by her pleas. He then dismisses her when he hears a knock at the door, perhaps in order to protect her from his own destructiveness or perhaps he has already decathected her.

The second scene of Act II opens with Caesar awakening to the tempest. Caesar recalls:

> Nor heaven nor earth have been at peace to-night.
> Thrice hath Calpurnia in her sleep cried out,
> 'Help ho: they murder Caesar!' (II.ii.1–3)

He asks the priests of the Roman gods to offer sacrifices and to inform him of how his plans will carry. Calpurnia enters and entreats him not to leave the house on this day, the Ides of March. He answers boldly that he is not afraid and that what rebels do behind his back they will cease doing when he shows his face. He feels his look would stop them and here reveals a weakness of a narcissistic kind. Calpurnia tells him:

> When beggars die there are no comets seen;
> The heavens themselves blaze forth the death of Princes.
> (II.ii.30–31)

Caesar responds that that is true for others, but for him:

> Cowards die many times before their deaths;
> The valiants never taste of death but once. (II.ii.32–33)

For Caesar, it seems, bravery is more important than status. The priests tell Caesar not to go to the forum, but he sees this as cowardice conduct for one such as he. The offerings to the gods are ominous:

> Plucking the entrails of an offering forth,
> They could not find a heart within the beast. (II.ii.39–40)

Caesar will soon supply the heart for his own sacrifice. Calpurnia tells him her dream and he repeats it to the trickster Decius.

> She dreamt tonight she saw my statua
> Which, like a fountain with an hundred spouts,
> Did run pure blood; and many lusty Romans
> Came smiling and did bathe their hands in it. (II.ii.76–79)

Decius, true to his word about how to catch a unicorn and other mythological beasts, engages Caesar with his alternative interpretation:

> It was a vision, fair and fortunate.
> Your statue spouting blood in many pipes

> In which so many smiling Romans bathed
> Signifies that from you great Rome shall suck
> Reviving blood, and that great men shall press
> For tinctures, stains, relics and cognisance. (II.ii.84–89)

Caesar is then father and, like the she wolf that suckled Romulus and Remus, also the mother of Rome. The conspirators arrive to take Caesar to the senate. This is only one of the two brief exchanges Brutus has with Caesar throughout the play. Caesar asks: "What is 't o'clock?" (II.ii.114). To which Brutus responds ominously: "Caesar, 'tis strucken eight" (II.ii.114). Decius further tempts Caesar, saying that once again the crown will be offered to him and he would appear cowardly if he put it off until Calpurnia has better dreams. Caesar's narcissism is again revealed. He dismisses Calpurnia in a similar fashion as Brutus did Portia. Caesar offers them wine:

> Good friends, go in, and taste some wine with me,
> And we, like friends, will straightway go together. (II.ii.126–127)

This touches momentarily on the universality of the theme of cannibalism. Unknowingly, Caesar metaphorically offers them to drink his blood. This too seems to function as Caesar offering himself as an introject for the conspirators to assimilate into their internal worlds.

The next scene introduces Artemidorus, who composes a letter he intends to give to Caesar on his way to the forum, warning him and naming the plotters. This parallels the story in Plutarch but adapted by Shakespeare. In Plutarch, it is Brutus' mother, Servilia, who gives Caesar a love letter on the way to the senate, rather than Artemidorus (Plutach, 1579, p. 247). Cato chides Caesar for reading personal letters instead of attending to the senate business. Caesar here says to Artemidorus: "What touches us ourself shall be last served" (III.i.8). While the paternity of Brutus is left out of the play, Caesar has treated him with high regard and has helped him achieve significant positions in the Roman government. He promoted Brutus above the more experienced Cassius, as First Praetor and would have named him his heir.

It is now 9 a.m. At the capital, Artemidorus presses his letter into Caesar's hand. It remains unread. Seeing the soothsayer, Caesar says to him: "The Ides of March are come" (III.i.1). The soothsayer replies to his boast: "Ay Caesar but not gone" (II.i.2). Meanwhile the conspirators as a group ask Caesar to return Publius Cimber from banishment. Comparing himself to the northern star, Caesar replies:

> The skies are painted with unnumber'd sparks;
> They are all fire, and every one doth shine;
> But there's but one in all doth hold his place.
> So in the world: 'tis furnish'd well with men,
> And men are flesh and blood, and apprehensive.
> Yet in number I do know but one
> That unassailable holds on his rank
> Unshaked of motion. And I am he. (III.i.63–70)

This is indeed hubris, the flaw of pride, which leads Caesar to his death. When Brutus also kneels and asks Caesar to change his mind, Caesar is astonished. When another conspirator asks Caesar to rescind the exile, Caesar says: "Hence, wilt thou lift up Olympus?" (III.i.75). If Brutus is not successful how could anyone else expect to move Caesar? With the image of Olympus, Caesar's identification with the gods is complete. Caska stabs him, and the frenzied hacking begins.

On stage, as Caesar is struck he looks at Brutus and says: "Et tu, Brute! Then fall Caesar" (III.i.77). Caesar throws his cloak over his head. Despite being murdered, it is as if Caesar chooses his own moment to die and is not passive even in his death. The audience, having read Plutarch, knows that he is Caesar's son (Plutarch, 1579, p. 274). Here Caesar sees Brutus as if he is his son, moving it from rumour to fantasy. Caesar protects him although Brutus fought for Pompey in the civil war. Thus, while the contemporary audience sees the murder as a terrible betrayal, the Elizabethan audience understood the play to be of a patricide.

As soon as the murder is committed, Cinna and Cassius start shouting slogans of freedom and liberty (III.i.78). Brutus tries to calm the populace with "Ambition's debt is paid" (III.i.83). Publius, an older senator, is immobilised by the confusion and is instructed by Brutus that no more blood will be shed, revealing how little Brutus understands anything about the murder. Cassius, who is more realistic, and in touch with the politics of a coup d'état says:

> And leave us, Publius, lest that the people
> Rushing on us, should do your age some mischief. (III.i.92–93)

Cassius is concerned about Antony and is told that he has returned home during this time of confusion. Brutus now seems to be undergoing dramatic changes. He rationalises Caesar's death in a style like the other conspirators. If man knows that he will die, he begins to worry about how he will face death. By this logic they did Caesar a favour by ending his anxiety about death, thus they that killed him were his friends. Brutus' language now sounds more like Cassius':

> So are we Caesar's friends that have abridged
> His time of fearing death. (III.i.104–105)

Interrupting himself mid line, Brutus falls apart as he shouts:

> Stoop, Romans, stoop.
> And let us bathe our hands in Caesar's blood
> Up to the elbows and besmear our swords.
> then walk we forth even to the marketplace,
> And waving our red weapons o'er our heads let's all cry,
> 'Peace, Freedom and Liberty.' (III.i.105–110)

For Brutus, the end is the death of Caesar. He has no plans for what will occur next, and the future he refers to is fantasy. Cassius is a true plotter and knows there will be a power vacuum and someone will be needed to fill it. He understands that he must get the populace on his side using the reputation of "Honourable Brutus" to accomplish this. The father–son bond between Caesar and Brutus is apparent but not manifestly acknowledged. Perhaps the patricidal element may be so frightening that even Shakespeare omitted the overt references.

As Brutus fragments, Cassius also undergoes changes. Cassius is very conscious about being upstaged and his rage is now beginning to be transferred to Brutus, while simultaneously he needs Brutus for the coup. Cassius says:

> Stoop, then, and wash. How many ages hence
> Shall this our lofty scene be acted over
> In states unborn and accents yet unknown! (III.i.111–113)

Cassius appeases the audience, inviting us into the conspiracy with the sense that we are privileged to be watching an historical event and as such it cannot be an interpersonal one. Brutus, too, says: "How many times shall Caesar bleed in sport ..." (III.i.114). Each draws us in. Each has a different reason for opposing Caesar. We too have blood on our hands and are perhaps the worst of the villains, as we have no motivation.

Antony is politic. He sends his servant ahead to ensure his safety, bearing the message:

> Say I love Brutus and I honour him.
> Say I feared Caesar, honoured him and loved him. (III.i.128–129)

Caesar, he both loved and feared, while Brutus he only loves, as Brutus is not thought to be powerful enough to fear. Antony enters and his language changes from a statesman's grief into a personal loss. Antony is mourning. He notices the blood on the conspirators' arms:

> Now, whilst your purple hands do reek and smoke,
> Fulil your pleasure, live a thousand years,
> I shall not find myself so apt to die. (III.i.158–160)

Antony says he will fall with Caesar. Brutus defends their actions and tells Antony that Antony is safe: "To you our swords have leaden points ..." (III.i.173). Cassius invites Antony to join them as an equal. He does not recognise that Antony needs to metabolise the loss. Brutus, in a traumatic state, is better able to speak to Antony: "Why I that did love Caesar when I struck him ..." (III.i.182). Antony shakes their still bloodied hands and asks their reason for the assassination. Now all on stage have Caesar's purple blood on their hands. Antony resembles a conspirator, but pushes on in questioning them. Antony says: "My credit now stands on such slippery ground ..." (III.i.191). His protector is dead and he is literally standing on his blood. To Caesar's body Antony laments:

> Had I as many eyes as thou hast wounds,
> Weeping as fast as they stream forth thy blood ... (III.i.200–201)

The conspirator, he continues: "... Signed in thy spoil and crimsoned in thy Lethe" (III.i.206). Lethe, the waters of forgetfulness in Hades, is ironically evoked as Antony will not forget.

Cassius presses Antony to join them, now speaking in a more militaristic fashion. Meanwhile, Brutus has fallen back into denial of his rageful and murderous impulses. Brutus, with his arms bloody, says:

> Or else were this a savage spectacle.
> Our reason are so full of good regard
> That were you, Antony, the son of Caesar,
> You should be satisfied. (III.i.223–226)

Brutus compels Antony to imagine himself as the son of Caesar, thus projecting his relationship onto Antony. Brutus promises to tell Antony why they killed Caesar. While Brutus will let Antony speak at the funeral, Cassius recognises the danger in this. Antony may speak after Cassius and Brutus and he must emphasise that he speaks with their permission. Brutus brushes the doubts aside just as Caesar did the soothsayer. Brutus is becoming like Caesar. As described in "Mourning and Melancholia" (Freud, 1917e, pp. 243–258), Brutus identifies with the lost object by becoming like Caesar. Alone with Caesar's corpse Antony says:

> Woe to the hand that shed this costly blood.
> Over thy wounds now do I prophesy
> (Which like dumb mouths do ope their ruby lips
> To beg the voice and utterance of my tongue). (III.i.259–262)

Antony's words will turn Caesar's wounds to mouths and his utterance will incite rebellion. Antony apologies to Caesar's corpse for acting so passively. He prophesises a bloody war to avenge Caesar's death. Antony's rising rhythms reveal his blood lust. Like a rising tide, each line stands atop the previous until he says:

> That mothers shall but smile when they behold
> Their infants quartered with the hands of war:
> All pity choked with custom of fell deeds,
> And Caesar's spirit, ranging for revenge,
> With Ate by his side come hot from hell,
> Shall in these confines, with a monarch's voice,
> Cry havoc and let slip the dogs of war,
> That this foul deed shall smell above the earth
> With carrion men, groaning for burial. (III.i.267–275)

Evoking Ate, the goddess of blood and strife, Antony's "carrion men" continue the earlier metaphors in the play, of dogs, the hunt, and the hunted. The hunt changes to the revenge of the hunted and its innocent victims will be avenged. Antony immediately sends a message to Octavius, Caesar's heir, to wait until summoned before returning to Rome. Brutus' eulogy is careful and measured and convinces the crowd that it was for the greater good. Brutus says:

> ... not that I loved Caesar less, but that I loved
> Rome more. (III.ii.21–22)

The language of love is reminiscent of Freud's later instinct theory—that is, Eros and Thanatos. Here it is used by Brutus, not in a way to accept both as inevitable parts of the human experience, but to elevate death as the superior instinct. Freud initially conceptualised psychological motivation in terms of an interplay between the self-preservative instincts of the ego and the libido. He later revised this theory, arguing that the ego's self-preservative instincts derived their energy from a transformation of object libido into narcissistic libido. Freud later reframed psychological motivation in terms of a life instinct (Eros) and a death instinct (Thanatos) (Freud, 1920g, pp. 7–61). Thanatos is that which Brutus here champions.

Antony then enters, dragging Caesar's body. He begins his oration:

> Friends, Romans, countrymen, lend me your ears:
> I come to bury Caesar, not to praise him.
> The evil that men do lives after them:
> The good is oft interred with their bones.
> So let it be with Caesar. The noble Brutus
> Hath told you Caesar was ambitious:
> If it were so, it was a grievous fault,
> And grievously hath Caesar answer'd it. (III.ii.74–81)

Speaking with shorter words and more speed Antony continues:

> Did this in Caesar seem ambitious?
> When that the poor have cried, Caesar hath wept:
> Ambition should be made of sterner stuff. (III.ii.91–93)

Antony essentially says: You should be mourning his loss, instead of siding with his murderers. As with Caesar's use of his seizure (or psuedo-seizure) to stir the people, Antony utilises real emotion for political advantage:

> My heart is in the coffin there with Caesar,
> And I must pause till it come back to me. (III.ii.107–108)

In a grand gesture he begins to weep and descends from the dais in an action that is as dramatic as Caesar's seizure, and shows that he did learn from him.

Antony then holds Caesar's testament, which he refuses to read, saying that it will turn the people away from the rebels. Instead he picks up the bloodstained cloak that Caesar was wearing, recalling that Caesar put it on for the first time in Spain after a great victory. He then describes each hole in the garment, naming each assassin who plunged his sword though it and into Caesar's body. Of Brutus, Antony says:

> For Brutus, as you know, was Caesar's angel.
> Judge, O you gods, how dearly Caesar loved him.
> This was the most unkindest cut of all … (III.ii.179–181)

While attempting to rouse a mob, this also reflects Antony's jealousy of Brutus. He then reads the will in which Caesar leaves money to every Roman citizen, and gives his estates to the people. Antony adds the word "treason" subtly and then works up to the word "traitors". The momentum of the oration indicates Antony's excitement as he stirs the people to action. Antony says:

> But were I Brutus,
> And Brutus Antony, there were an Antony
> Would ruffle up your spirits and put a tongue
> In every wound of Caesar that should move
> The Stones of Rome to rise and mutiny. (III.ii.219–223)

Again Brutus and Antony are held next to one another. When the mob rush out to kill the conspirators and burn their houses, Antony merely lets events take their course. Time surprises us again as Octavius, who is some years' distance away, has arrived by the closing of Antony's speech. We are allowed some insight into Octavius' character, as he rushes to Rome and does not wait for Antony to summon him. Brutus and Cassius have fled Italy after hearing the effect of the oration, in which language itself turns the Roman citizens into a vengeful mob.

The poet Cinna, having the same name as a conspirator, is torn to pieces on stage by the crowd. Someone calls out that even if he is not a rebel he should be killed for his poor verses. While it is a bit of humour, this murder of Cinna is also an example of the terror and bloodletting that follows a counter-coup. While all of Shakespeare's plays have, at various times, been altered or taken in and out of repertoire, *Julius Caesar* has been continually performed since the restoration—the death of Cinna is the only scene that was routinely cut from productions for hundreds of years. The re-inclusion of it was in a New York production in 1937 (Daniell, 1998, pp. 99–121). Perhaps World War I made the audience more ready to accept the bloodiness, the corruption, and the desperation for victory.

At the start of Act IV, Antony, Octavius and Lepidus are preparing a list of those who will be put to death for siding with the conspirators. These include the brother of Lepidus and Antony's nephew. The three have become the triumvirs now ruling Rome. We know from history that 300 senators were killed, including Cicero, as well as 3,000 citizens thought to be allied with the rebels. In this scene Antony proves to be the greatest of plotters when he tells Octavius that they will get rid of Lepidus when they have no further use of him. Citing his age and experience he also tries to intimidate the young Octavius. He will execute anyone he suspects without benefit of trial and even changes Caesar's will so that the money, which was to be given to the citizens, is instead to be used to raise an army to pursue Brutus and Cassius.

The next scene is in the army camp in Sardis. Brutus confronts Cassius with his corruption. To which Cassius responds:

> I am a soldier, I
> Older in practice, abler than yourself
> To make conditions. (IV.iii.30–32)

Cassius then realises he has said too much and attempts to undo it, saying: "I said, an elder soldier, not a better" (IV.iii.56). He adds: "You love me not" (IV.iii.88). Love now means something different to Cassius—it is no longer used to manipulate Brutus, but becomes a true affect. Brutus, however, has shifted from identifying with Eros to be identified with Thanatos. He responds: "I do not like your faults" (IV.iii.88). Intimately they share the line, as Cassius answers him: "A friendly eye could never see such faults" (IV.iii.89). He offers Brutus a dagger to kill him, saying jealously:

> Strike as thou didst at Caesar: for I know,
> When thou didst hate him worst, thou lov'dst him better
> Than ever thou lov'dst Cassius. (IV.iii.105–107)

Brutus agrees that he too was ill tempered and they embrace. They drink and Cassius says: "I cannot drink too much of Brutus' love" (IV.iii.160). This is reminiscent of the wine Caesar shared with his assassins before going to the senate, and the wine as a metaphoric introject for taking in aspects of the other. As at the senate, this too will prove a lethal exchange. In this play, the sharing of wine foreshadows the sharing of blood. Portia has suicided, eating blazing embers—but Brutus seems unmoved. Brutus then launches into his strategy to defeat Antony and Octavius at Philippi. The time is ripe, as the enemy is increasing its forces while the rebels are at the height of their power. Cassius is now in agreement with Brutus, and shares his money as he departs.

Brutus' deterioration is evident. He calls for his captains to sleep in his tent, as he cannot sleep. He is distracted and he mislays his book:

> Look, Lucius, here's the book I sought for so:
> I put it in the pocket of my gown. (IV.iii.250–251)

Lucius responds: "I was sure your lordship did not give it me" (IV.iii.252). Brutus says: "Bear with me, good boy, I am much forgetful" (IV.iii.253). As Lucius falls asleep, Brutus cannot find the page he left off reading. The ghost of Caesar enters as Brutus is most distracted. Brutus is in dread, as Hamlet will be later, when he sees the ghost of his murdered father. Brutus says:

> I think it is the weakness of mine eyes
> That shapes this monstrous apparition.
> It comes upon me: art thou any thing?
> Art thou some god, some angel, or some devil,
> That mak'st my blood cold, and my hair to stare?
> Speak to me what thou art. (IV.iii.274–279)

The ghost answers: "Thy evil spirit, Brutus" (IV.iii.274–279). And again collapsing the passage of time, the ghost says he will visit him at Philippi. Ghosts in Elizabethan literature are avengers who draw their guilty murderers to their death, as in the revenge tragedies. Once the guilty party is dead, the murdered ghost may rest. Shakespeare goes beyond the conventions of his time. Ghosts, for Shakespeare, are aspects of guilty conscience. Brutus, who does not believe in the Roman gods, must now deal with his own guilt for the murder. He can no longer rationalise or deny it. He is the slayer of the father who loved and protected him. Killing the father did not give him "liberty" or "freedom" but has only given him self-torture and death in his internal world.

The final act begins at Philippi, at the camp of Antony and Octavius. They discuss military strategy. We see a parallel rivalry between these two, as with Cassius and Brutus. Antony says:

> Octavius, lead your battle softly on,
> Upon the left hand of the even field. (V.i.16–17)

Octavius responds: "Upon the right hand I. Keep thou the left" (V.i.18). Antony says: "Why do you cross me in this exigent?" (V.i.19), to which Octavius warns: "I do not cross you: but I will do so" (V.i.20). Antony sets a plan that Octavius, showing his Caesarian character, contradicts; for Octavius is the heir, not Antony, and he flaunts it. Under a flag of truce, Antony awaits Brutus' explanation for the murder, which Brutus had promised him. Antony charges Brutus with having no justification for killing Caesar. Cassius reminds Brutus that he had wanted Antony to be slain along with Caesar. Unhearing Brutus says:

> But this same day
> Must end that work the Ides of March begun. (V.i.112–113)

We see the change in Cassius. The first storm he viewed as a natural occurrence. The second storm, however, suggests something different to him:

> Why now, blow wind, swell billow and swim bark.
> The storm is up and all is on the hazard. (V.i.66–67)

Cassius begins to see omens from the gods:

> ... Two mighty eagles fell and there they perched
> Gorging and feeding from our soldiers' hands,
> Who went to Philippi here consorted us:
> This morning are they fled away and gone,
> And in their steads do ravens, crows and kites
> Fly o'er our heads and downward look on us
> As we were sickly prey ... (V.i.80–86)

The hunter projects and sees himself as the hunted. Brutus, for his part, sees himself under the power of something mighty, but is doomed. His ambivalence towards Caesar, who loved him, prevents him from experiencing any type of victory. If he should die, it should be in battle as is fit for a soldier; yet, at some level, he simultaneously fears and believes that he deserves to be captured and humiliated by the Roman people. With these thoughts he bids farewell to Cassius. Cassius, too, says:

> This day I breathed first. Time is come round;
> And where I did begin, there I shall end.
> My life has run his compass. (V.iii.23–25)

Brutus sensing a weakness in Octavius' forces takes advantage and routes his army. Cassius seeing men in retreat blames Brutus for moving too swiftly. As Cassius suicides, he dies with Caesar's name on his lips:

> Caesar, thou art revenged
> Even with the sword that killed thee. (V.iii.45–46)

News comes that Antony's men are in Cassius' camp. The difference between life and death is only a change in tense from being to having been. Messala asks: "Is not that he?" (V.iii.58) speaking to Brutus to which Titinius responds: "No, this was he ..." (V.iii.59).

Error, technically, is both cause and effect. Messala reveals something of the Elizabethan view of melancholy beyond the medieval humours. Melancholy, he explains, breeds error. And error is a difficult offspring:

> O hateful Error, Melancholy's child,
> Why dost thou show to the apt thoughts of men

> The things that are not? O Error, soon conceived,
> Thou never com'st upon a happy birth
> But kill'st the mother that engender'd thee. (V.iii.66–70)

This metaphor is the only reference to a mother in the play. Titinius returns to tell of Brutus' victory but, finding Cassius dead, kills himself with rhyming couplet, as language itself must end.

> By your leave, gods. This is a Roman's part.
> Come, Cassius' sword, and find Titinius' heart. (V.iii.89–90)

On finding Cassius and Titinius dead, Brutus says:

> O Julius Caesar, though art mighty yet.
> Thy spirit walks abroad and turns our swords
> In our own proper entrails. (V.iii.94–96)

Caesar becomes powerful after his death, as an avenging spirit.

In the final scene Brutus is cornered. When Antony first saw Caesar dead he likened Caesar to a trapped deer. Now Brutus is the trapped animal. Brutus says:

> The ghost of Caesar hath appeared to me
> Two several times by night; at Sardis once,
> And this last night, here in Philippi fields:
> I know my hour is come. (V.v.7–10)

Brutus runs on his sword saying:

> Caesar, now be still.
> I killed not thee with half so good a will. (V.v.51–52)

Antony and Octavius enter and discover Brutus' body. Octavius promises to take all of Brutus' men into his service. Of Brutus, Antony eulogises:

> This was the noblest Roman of them all:
> All the conspirators save only he
> Did that they did in envy of great Caesar.

> He only, in a general honest thought
> And common good to all, made one of them. (V.v.71–75)

Antony continues, sounding like Theseus, describing the death of Oedipus as a man who braved even the gods themselves:

> His life was gentle, and the elements
> So mix'd in him that Nature might stand up
> And say to all the world, 'This was a man!' (V.v.69–71)

Octavius, the heir and future emperor, has the last word and calls for the proper funeral rites for Brutus.

Julius Caesar is a play that Harold Bloom suggested would be a better candidate for an oedipal tragedy than *Hamlet* (Bloom, 1998, pp. 104–118). Like Oedipus, Brutus kills Caesar, his presumptive father, and suffers the consequences for his act. The problem for classical psychoanalysis is the absence of the sexual drive toward the mother. Indeed, women are not stressed in this play. From the perspective of drive theory, this focus on the aggressive drive only and the de-emphasising of the sexual drive leaves us to wonder if we are dealing with aspects of narcissistic development. Writing from a self-psychological perspective, Terman (Terman, 1984, pp. 87–104) has re-conceptualised the Oedipus complex as a stage in the development from archaic to mature expressions of narcissism. Themes of rivalry and competition with an idealised father figure (e.g., Caesar) can be located within the context of the person's (e.g., Brutus') narcissistic strivings to establish a gendered sense of self as powerful, vigorous and assertive. The play's idealisation of Caesar is made evident through his self-aggrandisement into the polar star by which other men steer their course through life. His fearlessness (perhaps counter-phobic) and his certainty that he will live forever in the minds of men assures him immortality even as his aging deficits are revealed. He will die but once.

In contrast with the self-psychological perspective on narcissism as a primary developmental phenomenon, Andre Green (Green, 1986, pp. 115–141) suggests that narcissism might also function as a defence against the death instinct. With respect to Caesar's own narcissism, one might wonder if his own accomplishments are merely a defence against the loss of self, of which death represents. In support of this view, Caesar adds to the anti-dying retinue in the play by wanting Calpurnia to conceive a child during the fertility rites of the Lupercal.

Brutus is another matter. His primitive superego forbids frivolity. He has the high seriousness of a stoic and does not require the illusion of gods. He is in some way a scientific man beyond animism or religion. He lives in an inner world of fantasies, thoughts, and feelings. He is at one with the acts and ideas of his forebearers, such as the regicide Junius Brutus. His possible illegitimacy is unacceptable. His ambivalence is more concrete than in most father–son relationships. If the question of his legitimacy is a fantasy that Shakespeare keeps from us, it is real to Brutus and must be extricated. The kindness that Caesar shows him only feeds his rage and hatred. In our view, this drives the drama and not Cassius' seduction. He discounts Portia's wish to expiate his anger by her own self-castration. He can only be passive and accept Caesar's love, a homoerotic solution, or destroy Caesar and himself to be a true man. His is the most vulnerable self, which fragments after the murder. Oedipus unconsciously slew his father, Lauis, and married his mother, Jocasta. Servilia, Brutus' mother, is a devalued woman. Absent from the play, she is not his love object. Brutus is not a member of a primal horde although he joins the conspiracy. He becomes a true member after the murder of Caesar, when he bathes in his father's blood. As much as he may want to identify with Caesar as a warrior and as a classic writer, he is, unfortunately, unable to do so. If our lot in life is our ambivalence in relationships, Shakespeare suggests our inner world is a burdened private sphere that we must carry with us to our end.

CHAPTER FIVE

Madness and the death of self in *Titus Andronicus*

Titus Andronicus is a difficult play. Read, it feels disorderly and disorganising. Staged, it proves complicated, and with its grotesque imagery it is difficult to make palatable to contemporary audiences. While it was popular and a financial success during William Shakespeare's lifetime, it was abandoned and left virtually unperformed for three centuries. It continues to be one of the least popular of Shakespeare's works. Comments by some of the best readers of Shakespeare attest to this. Samuel Johnson described it as a work that "... can scarcely be conceived tolerable to any audience" (Johnson, 1864, p. 364). T. S. Eliot characterised it as "one of the stupidest and most uninspired plays ever written" (Eliot, 1950, p. 67). Harold Bloom states "I am rendered incredulous, and still wish that Shakespeare had not perpetuated this poetic atrocity" (Bloom, 1998, p. 79).

There have been many performances of Shakespeare using inventive staging and direction, which work hard to undo the difficulties of the content. Following Puck's example in his apology of *A Midsummer Night's Dream*: "... you have but slumber'd here/While these visions did appear" (V.i.411–412), The American Players Theater, for instance, to make palatable the misogynist sentiments in *The Taming of the Shrew* produced the play as if it were all a drunken dream of Kate's henpecked

115

husband Petruchio. In 1996, the slightly abridged film *Titus* framed the story in a manner that also protects the audience from its alarming content. It begins with a boy playing with toy soldiers, set up as marching men, which are sent flying by the child's destructiveness. The marching men become Titus' army, but since it is introduced in the context of kinderspiel the events that follow need not be taken seriously, or perhaps the viewer may revert to viewing this as imaginative play when the drama becomes too painful.

Unlike many of Shakespeare's plays, there is no source for *Titus Andronicus*. The play opens with dissension in the Roman court. The sons of the late emperor struggle for power. We are introduced to Saturninus, the eldest brother. Saturninus for Saturn is from the Greek god Kronos. Kronos, usually depicted with the scythe he had used to castrate his father, Uranus, was Gaia's youngest son, and he represented the first generations of the Titans. Known as the Roman god Saturn, he himself was overthrown by his own son Zeus. Irwin Rosen summarises the creation myth, writing that the children of Uranus and Gaia "… all (probably projectively) feared and hated by their father (Uranus), who kept them buried alive in the earth, or … inside the body of their mother … (Saturn) Kronos (the son) … castrate[d] Uranus and … seize[d] power; projectively fearing a subsequent revenge from his own offspring, he ate them at birth" (Rosen, 2007, pp. 595–620). This early primitive myth lends the name to Shakespeare's childless Saturninus, yet may prove to better identify the character of Titus in all his aspects and acts as a leitmotif of the father–son relationships throughout the play.

As the play opens Saturninus encourages his followers to:

> Plead my successive title with your swords.
> I am his first-born son that was the last
> That wore the imperial diadem of Rome. (I.i.4–6)

He believes violently that the title should be his. His call to arms allows us a glimpse into his inner life; his vanity and his aggression. On the other hand, Bassianus, Saturninus' younger brother, is more in tune with the people of Rome. He does not threaten with arms, but rather asks the Romans to use judgement, and emphasises the power of their vote.

> But let desert in pure election shine,
> And, Romans, fight for freedom in your choice. (I.i.16–17)

This struggle for power between these brothers is contrasted with the respectful exchange between Titus and his brother Marcus. Marcus, a tribune, welcomes his brother home, likening Titus to one of the legendary founders of Rome, Aeneas. Marcus refers to Titus as "… Chosen Andronicus, surnamed Pius …" (I.i.23). By linking Titus to Aeneas he invokes the image of a devout and patriotic man. Titus Andronicus is a soldier. He has successfully battled on the borders of the Roman Empire some forty years. For him, murder and disorder are not simply necessary, but celebrated on the battlefield, as these deaths protect the order of Rome, and serve to warn the barbarous and disorderly others. Titus, newly returned from war with the Goths, enters Rome with great pomp, bearing with him his captives: Tamora, the Queen of the Goths, her three sons, and Aaron the Moor. Titus likens his return to Rome as to a ship:

> Lo, as the bark that hath discharged her fraught
> Returns with precious jading to the bay … (I.i.74–75)

In this first of many aquatic images, Titus is a boat, sailing upon the ocean. But the "precious" cargo that returns to Rome are not his surviving four sons, but the bodies of those many sons killed in battle. Lavinia, Titus' only daughter, cries tears of joy upon her father's return, and tears of sorrow for her lost brothers. She says: "Lo, at this tomb my tributary tears …" (I.i.162) both as a tribute to her brothers and the tributary river to the underworld. In reference to Virgil's Aeneas, Titus chides himself:

> Why suffer'st thou thy sons unburied yet
> To hover on the dreadful shore of Styx? (I.i.90–91)

Lucius, Titus' eldest surviving son, calls for a sacrifice of the Queen's eldest son; Alarbus is to be dismembered and his entrails burned. Initially this appears to be in obedience with Roman burial rituals and does not shock us. However, this claim for a religious ceremony is both suggested and undertaken by the sons of Titus thus displacing the priests, and inadvertently underlining its barbarity. When Tamora pleads to spare her son, Titus replies:

> Patient yourself, madam and pardon me.
> These are their brethren whom your Goths beheld
> Alive and dead, and for their brethren slain,
> Religiously they ask a sacrifice.
> To this your son is mark'd, and die he must,
> To appease their groaning shadows that are gone. (I.i.124–129)

It is a mistake to hear this as the moment of hubris. The death of Alarbus is a necessary ritual as punishment for all who would take arms against Rome, and as a means by which man "seeks to order and control his precarious and unstable world" (Palmer, 1972, pp. 320–339). For Rome is order and the land of the Goths, chaos. Titus omits the fact that the brethren he speaks of are his sons, and denies a personal wish for vengeance. We begin to doubt the piety of Titus. Beneath his patriotic exterior there may be a filicide, a man who, like Kronos/Saturn, kills his sons to eliminate potential rivals. Titus led his sons to death on the battlefield; a murderous instinct displaced and projected in a manner he can rationalise and defend against.

This scene, just 100 lines into the play, is often interpreted as justification for Tamora's revenge. If read this way, Tamora is not dissimilar from Heronimo's quest for vengeance for his son Horatio's death, in Thomas Kyd's *The Spanish Tragedy*. This would simply be a revenge tragedy. Once revenge enters that genre it almost necessitates the action of vengeance to become a character in itself. Much like the allegorical characters of the Middle Ages characters can now represent a pure human trait in an abstract and metaphorical way.

Tamora swears by her "mother's tears", (I.i.123) but there are no mothers for Titus, thus this has no meaning to him. There is no notice in the play of Titus' wife, neither are any Roman mothers mentioned. She is requesting a break in order, which Titus cannot contemplate. Titus does not become aware of Tamora's anger or anticipate her vengeance. Tamora is the primitive other who sees all women as devouring and destructive forces. The play can also be viewed as society's fear of the breakthrough of primitive, murderous impulses of the other; of the barbarian females, such as Euripides' *Medea*. For Tamora, to be defeated—to kneel and beg for her son's life—is so antithetical to our view of her, and to her view of herself. She is a character as much as she is revenge itself. Tamora is in stark contrast to Lavinia, who is the other female and Titus' virginal daughter. Titus' tenderness towards Lavinia is a vulnerability that will later be used against him in Tamora's revenge. Are we not close to Freud's anthropological view of the father who kept the women for himself and was killed and eaten by the band of brothers, the act of which left a mark on the unconscious of mankind? (Freud, 1912–1913, pp. 1–161) Freud and Shakespeare here seem to share this mythic prehistoric view of the birth of civilisation; order out of chaos and its great cost to mankind.

For a play without mother characters, Titus shows us glimpses of the "maternal" elements in himself. Placing his dead sons into the crypt, for instance, Titus almost sings to them, as if to comfort them with a lullaby.

> In peace and honour rest you here, my sons;
> Rome's readiest champions, repose you here in rest,
> Secure from worldly chances and mishaps.
> Here lurks no treason, here no envy swells,
> Here grow no damned grudges; here are no storms,
> No noise, but silence and eternal sleep:
> In peace and honour rest you here, my sons. (I.i.151–157)

This soft monologue is a contrast to the warrior just met.

At this junction in the play, Marcus announces that the people's choice for emperor is his brother. Titus, like Coriolanus, knows that he is a soldier and not a statesman. He refuses to recognise the legitimacy of choice by the people. In a similar situation, Coriolanus scorns and insults the plebeians. Titus, however, appears thoughtful in his response, saying:

> A better head her glorious body fits
> Than his that shakes for age and feebleness.
> What, should I don this robe and trouble you?
> Be chosen with proclamations to-day,
> To-morrow yield up rule, resign my life
> And set abroad new business for you all? (I.i.190–195)

Titus seems to believe in law and order, and also in primogeniture, more fiercely than choice or public gratitude. He continues:

> Rome, I have been thy soldier forty years,
> And led my country's strength successfully,
> And buried one and twenty valiant sons,
> Knighted in field, slain manfully in arms
> In right and service of their noble country:
> Give me a staff of honour for mine age,
> But not a sceptre to control the world. (I.i.193–199)

This latter statement foreshadows the first scene in *King Lear*, when Lear too wishes to relinquish his rule. The difference is that Titus says he "shakes for age and feebleness", acknowledging his infirmity but denying the primacy of his drives and that his drives have not diminished with age. Titus refuses to serve as emperor. Saturninus, deeply humiliated shouts: "Andronicus, would thou wert shipped to hell …" (I.i.210). Titus quickly seems to lose the action part of his character. Despite Saturninus' ruthlessness and threats of violence to Rome and to Titus, Titus chooses him over his brother Bassianus.

Titus, using a metaphor of mother and child declares:

> Content thee, prince; I will restore to thee
> The people's hearts, and wean them from themselves.
> (I.i.214–215)

Titus knows that Saturninus feels slighted, but believes he can somehow make it up to him by having the people love Saturninus as emperor. Titus understands part of what motivates Saturninus but mistakenly believes he can undo the injury. Titus makes a dangerous choice in Saturninus.

In his address to the people of Rome in nominating Saturninus, Titus references the golden age of Saturn/Kronos:

> Reflect on Rome as Titan's rays on earth,
> And ripen justice in this commonweal. (I.i.230–231)

This sounds like the stuff of comedies, if only Titus didn't believe him. There is now a loss of justice and reason. Titus, in respect for the new emperor, gives Saturninus his sword, chariot, and prisoners, and thus discharges his responsibilities as soldier. Saturninus asks Titus for his daughter's hand in marriage. This was a common way for enemies to reconcile, as with Prince Balthazar in *The Spanish Tragedy*, or with Queen Elizabeth, as she dangled her suitors with the possibility of a union with their countries. As with all Saturninus' gestures it is unclear what his intentions are. Lavinia is betrothed to his younger brother Bassianus. Marcus accepts this arrangement with Bassianus as do Titus' sons. Titus is beside himself and shouts:

> Traitors, avaunt! Where is the emperor's guard?
> Treason, my lord! Lavinia is surprised! (I.i.286–287)

This break in order—that his own children are disobedient—is a terrible affront to Titus. His son Mutius bars his way, and Titus kills him easily. Is it simply order and honour that he is defending? Titus exhibits his sadism in murdering Mutius, with his easy rationalisation that his sons dishonour him and therefore he can slay them. We are at the beginning of the Oedipus complex in which the father plots to kill his son (the infant Oedipus) for fear that he will do away with him (Freud, 1910h, pp. 165–175).

> Nor thou, nor he, are any sons of mine;
> My sons would never so dishonour me.
> Traitor, restore Lavinia to the emperor (I.i.294–296)

And Lucius responds:

> Dead if you will, but not to be his wife,
> That is another's lawful promised love. (I.i.297–298)

Off the battlefield Titus is now waging war in the court. Here, however, he cannot be the one who commands. He attempts to bar his sons from burying Mutius, but backs down—perhaps as a result of Lucius. Lucius attempts to restore Titus' self-esteem saying: "Dear father, soul and substance of us all ..." (I.i.379). Is this a kernel of what Lear needs to energise his failing powers when he requires a love test of his daughters? Now the staging changes; Saturninus appears above the stage and Titus is below. Saturninus' hatred explodes. The act of making him emperor does not undo Titus as a paranoid projection for Saturninus, nor can Titus killing his own son undo the injury Saturninus suffers. He has recognised the jealousy in Saturninus but does not appreciate its quality. He cannot understand what he needs to know about himself and his relationship to others.

Shakespeare makes use of madness and feigned madness in his tragedies. Titus goes mad like Lear, Othello, Hamlet, and Macbeth, but unlike the others, Titus' revenge takes the place of both his madness and his sanity. In that plotting of revenge, Hamlet and Titus dissemble and pretend to be mad as a subterfuge to further their elaborate revenge schemes. Our usual scheme of symptom formation according to Freud (Freud, 1913i, pp. 317–326) is that a perceived slight or loss leads to manifest regression that can be relieved by fantasy formation of a wishful variety that brings the person back to "normalcy." But for those who are preconditioned or unable to use this manifest regression, repression proper emerges and revivifies and energises the archaic objects, part object, or selfobjects. If this regression does not find attachments in the external world through transferences, one falls into a death-like state—described by Hamlet:

> How weary, stale, flat and unprofitable,
> Seem to me all the uses of this world! (I.ii.135–136)

Hamlet uses the word "seem" and thus it is a depressive description, for one in this state—so devoid of objects—the world IS flat. The return from psychosis requires the employment of pseudo-objects, which give the appearance of energy but cannot be sustained.

In the tragedies of Titus and of Hamlet, Shakespeare suggests another device in the recovery from psychosis, namely a plan for revenge that quickens one's mind and makes one exquisitely aware of the motives of others. Dissembling and subterfuges are the products of such restitutive phenomenon. It is akin to "kernel of truth" in the paranoid's projections, but in these tragedies (more cruelly in Titus than in Hamlet) revenge works as an organiser for the profoundly fragmented self.

For us as audience, the killing of Mutius undoes his rationalisation that his twenty-one sons died for Rome, but may instead expose his unconscious wish to kill his male progeny; a wish that may break forth and drive him mad. Shakespeare does not agree with us, but restores Titus' relationship with his living sons and he buries Mutius appropriately. He address himself:

> Titus, when wert thou wont to walk alone
> Dishonoure'd thus and challenged of wrongs? (I.i.344–345)

He needs to evoke his own name in attempts at restoration, to remind himself who he is, or, more terrible, that he is.

In Act II the action moves from the court to the forest, where earthly and human nature may play out. Titus says:

> I have been troubled in my sleep this night,
> But dawning day new comfort hath inspired. (II.ii.9–10)

It is as if the events of Act I were a bad dream from which he has awakened, and all the threatening personages have returned to a seemingly harmonious order as Titus fantasises about the new day:

> And I have horse will follow where the game
> Makes way and runs like swallows o'er the plain. (II.ii.23–24)

He is unaware that it is his children who are the hunted.

Tamora plans with Aaron the Moor to have Bassianus killed and to have Titus' sons blamed for the murder. She also increases the revenge by having her sons rape Lavinia. Tamora's view of nature is not as orderly as Titus'. She says:

> Here never shines the sun, here nothing breeds
> Unless the nightly owl or fatal raven.
> And when they show'd me this abhorred pit,
> They told me here at dead time of the night
> A thousand fiends, a thousand hissing snakes,
> Ten thousand swelling toads, as many urchins,
> Would make such fearful and confused cries
> As any mortal body hearing it
> Should straight fall mad or else die suddenly. (II.iii.96–104)

For Tamora there is only night and the sun does nothing to dispel her dark motives or give her any comfort as the day offers Titus. Following up on her plans she states to her sons:

> Therefore away with her and use her as you will:
> The worse to her, the better loved of me. (II.iii.166–167)

And like the queen of the night in *The Magic Flute*, when she demands her daughter Pamina slay Sarastro, Tamara says:

> Revenge it as you love your mother's life,
> Or be ye not henceforth call'd my children. (II.iii.114–115)

She continues with reference to the spleen, her lust for the Moor, and her sons' aggressive lust for Lavinia:

> Farewell, my sons; see that you make her sure.
> Ne'er let my heart know merry cheer indeed
> Till all the Andronici be made away.
> Now will I hence to seek my lovely Moor,
> And let my spleenful sons this trull deflow'r. (II.iii.187–191)

When Lavinia pleads with Tamora to save her, the Queen of the Goths rebukes her as she was rebuked by Titus when she begged for her son's life. Tamora says:

> So should I rob my sweet sons of their fee
> No, let them satisfy their lust on thee. (II.iii.179–180)

Tamora foreshadows Lavinia's silence. Tamora says: "And whilst the babbling echo mocks the hounds" (II.iii.17). Echo, in mythology, is the disembodied voice of a nymph, and Lavinia will become the opposite of Echo; she will be a nymph without a voice. Lavinia's last spoken line is cut short. A curse aborted: "Confusion fall" (II.iii.184).

An Elizabethan idea of character formation was that it was nursed from the mother, by being suckled at her breast. In *Coriolanus*, his mother boasts her milk makes Coriolanus a great warrior. In pleading with Chiron and Demetrius, Lavinia hopelessly says:

When did the tiger's young ones teach the dam?

Admonishing the sons:

> "O, do not learn her wrath: she taught it thee."
> The milk thou suck'dst from her did turn to marble;
> Even at thy teat thou hadst thy tyranny. (II.iii.143–145)

After they have killed Bassianus, Chiron directs:

> Drag hence her husband to some secret hole
> And make his dead trunk pillow to our lust. (II.iii.129–130)

Lavinia is then raped in a dark pit in the forest, described as whose:

> ... mouth is covered with rude-growing briers
> Upon whose leaves are drops of new-shed blood ...
> (II.iii.199–200)

It is also described as an "... unhallowed and blood-stained hole ..." (II.iii.210), and a "detested, dark, blood-drinking pit" (II.iii.224) and "... the ragged entrails of this pit"' (II.ii.230). In these descriptions the pit itself becomes the body:

> ... this fell devouring receptacle
> As hateful as Cocytus' misty mouth. (II.iii.235–236)

Referring here again to the river in hell, the metaphor expands. The descriptions continue:

> ... the swallowing womb
> Of this deep pit, poor Bassianus' grave. (II.iii.239–240)

The entombment of Bassianus is no longer the mother's lullaby of the crypt in Act I. The pit is a bloody hole that takes men in and murders them in hymeneal blood. It is a pit of death, and a concretisation of the phallic and engulfing destructive women that Shakespeare personifies through Tamora's imagery, speeches, and actions. It is also Uranus devouring his sons.

After the rape, they cut off Lavinia's hands and tongue and she runs away. When Titus appears and discovers that his two sons have been arrested for murder he does not plead for their lives but asks for a trial and justice. We are almost fooled by the symmetry; Tamora begs for son's life, Alarbus dismembered, Lavinia dismembered, Titus begs for sons' lives. But again that is not this play. Titus is truly deluded when he asks Saturninus:

> ... I beg this boon with tears not lightly shed:
> That this fell fault of my accursed sons,
> Accursed if the fault be proved in them ... (II.iii.289–291)

He pleads:

> I did, my lord, yet let me be their bail,
> For by my fathers' reverend tomb I vow
> They shall be ready at your highness' will
> To answer their suspicion with their lives. (II.iii.295–298)

The difficulty here is that Titus is still clinging to a Rome with rules of law that no longer exist to an emperor who is waiting for a vehicle for his vengeance.

Act II ends with Marcus' discovery of Lavinia, and he notes her inability to name the perpetrators of the sadistic deed:

> Sorrow concealed, like an oven stopp'd,
> Doth burn the heart to cinders where it is. (II.iv.36–37)

This is a sophisticated precursor to Anna O's description of her need to reveal her sorrows through the talking cure and her "chimney-sweeping" (Freud & Breuer, 1895d, p. 30).

As Act III opens, Titus no longer asks for justice or even questions the guilt or innocence of his sons, but is mourning. Titus goes from viewing himself as a ship in Act I to becoming its cargo.

> O earth, I will befriend thee more with rain
> That shall distil from these two ancient urns
> Than youthful April shall with all his showers.
> In summer's drought I'll drop upon thee still;

> In winter with warm tears I'll melt the snow
> And keep eternal spring-time on thy face,
> So thou refuse to drink my dear sons' blood. (III.i.16–22)

Here he is at his most human self, arousing pity in the audience. When Lucius, who is to be banished, replies that there is no one left to hear his pleas and that his father is merely recounting his sorrows to a stone (III.i.29) Titus responds with a true insight:

> Why, 'tis no matter, man: if they did hear,
> They would not mark me, or if they did mark,
> They would not pity me; yet plead I must ... (III.i.33–35)

He continues his monologue with a profound sense of hopelessness and emptiness.

> Therefore I tell my sorrows to the stones,
> Who, though they cannot answer my distress,
> Yet in some sort they are better than the tribunes
> For that they will not intercept my tale.
> When I do weep, they humbly at my feet
> Receive my tears and seem to weep with me,
> And were they but attired in grave weeds
> Rome could afford no tribunes like to these.
> A stone is soft as wax, tribunes more hard than stones;
> A stone is silent and offendeth not,
> And tribunes with their tongues doom men to death.
> (III.i.37–47)

Titus here uses a rock as a selfobject and as an attempt at self-restoration. The stones will be consistent, will listen, and will feel empathic to him as they "seem to weep".

Marcus is concerned for his brother, who is unaware of Lavinia's plight, and also recognises this shattering catastrophic loss of objects, saying:

> One hour's storm will drown the fragrant meads:
> What will whole months of tears thy father's eyes? (II.iv.54–55)

Here Marcus likens Titus' suffering to drowning the fields. Soon Lavinia appears, and these scenes seem to lead to changes in both Titus and the audience, as if we watch the final scenes from afar. At the sight of Lavinia, Titus explains this is beyond what he could tolerate:

> What fool hath added water to the sea,
> Or brought a faggot to bright-burning Troy?
> My grief was at the height before thou camest,
> And now like Nilus it disdaineth bounds. (III.i.69–72)

As the Nile overflows so will he. The madness begins with a projection of his internal world to the natural world in which the sea will devour him but then he becomes the sea.

> When heaven doth weep, doth not the earth o'erflow?
> If the winds rage, doth not the sea wax mad,
> Threatening the welkin with his big-swoln face?
> And wilt thou have a reason for this coil?
> I am the sea. Hark how her sighs do blow.
> She is the weeping welkin, I the earth.
> Then must my sea be moved with her sighs,
> Then must my earth with her continual tears
> Become a deluge overflow'd and drown'd. (III.i.222–230)

This metaphor of water expands with the play until the tears from the first scene threaten to drown the whole world.

Titus asks Lavinia:

> Or shall we cut away our hands like thine?
> Or shall we bite our tongues and in dumb shows
> Pass the remainder of our hateful days? (III.i.131–133)

Titus, like Hamlet, is unable to act. But the similarity ends there. Hamlet is unable to act from unconscious conflicts over parricide and his remaining conflictual relationship with Gertrude. Titus is unable to act now, as his previous murders break though, and also he is rendered paralysed by the acts others visited upon him. The action he contemplates is to become like Lavinia and be devoid of tongue and hands, a concretised version of Freud's observation of mourning losses (Freud, 1917e, pp. 243–258). Later he will sacrifice his hand to the wily Moor. But not his tongue. This action moves towards revenge. Even as he receives the heads of his sons and his severed hand he is plotting to destroy Rome and sends his other son to raise an army among the Goths. Titus, at last, realises: "… That Rome is but a wilderness of tigers …" (III.i.54). At first, his action is purely psychotic. He appeals to the gods by shooting arrows with his grievances written upon them. With a metre that reminds one of Ophelia's mad scene, Titus addresses the arrows much like Ophelia addresses the flowers in *Hamlet*. Ophelia begins:

> There's fennel for you, and columbines: there's rue
> for you; and here's some for me … (IV.v.178–179)

Titus hands out his arrows:

> 'Ad Jovem', that's for you; here, 'Ad Apollinem:'
> 'Ad Martem', that's for myself:
> Here, boy, to Pallas; here, to Mercury;
> To Saturn, Caius—not to Saturnine:
> You were as good to shoot against the wind.
> To it, boy; Marcus, loose when I bid.
> Of my word, I have written to effect:
> There's not a god left unsolicited. (IV.iii.54–61)

He wants his henchmen to dig to Pluto's realm.

> 'Tis you must dig with mattock and with spade,
> And pierce the inmost centre of the earth.
> Then, when you come to Pluto's region,
> I pray you deliver him this petition. (IV.iii.11–14)

He would dig to the centre of the earth to find Pluto and ask for help, for the gods are no longer abstract beings but have specific habitations that can be reached but will be found empty. He looks to earth:

> What, wilt thou kneel with me?
> Do then, dear heart, for heaven shall hear our prayers,
> Or with our sighs we'll breathe the welkin dim

> And stain the sun with fog, as sometime clouds
> When they do hug him in their melting bosoms. (III.i.210–214)

He moves from the deities to nature and finds nature lifeless as well. There is a scene in which a child kills a fly. Titus begins by empathising with the fly, he asks: "Did it have parents?" There is an uncharacteristic break in the rhythm of the play. We are reminded of a friend's experience speaking with a child holocaust survivor. As our friend swatted a fly, the child asked: "Doesn't the fly have a right to live like any other creature?" In *Titus Andronicus* the boy responds to the admonition by saying:

> Pardon me, sir; it was a black ill-favour'd fly,
> Like to the empress' Moor. Therefore I kill'd him. (III.ii.67–68)

Now Titus attacks the fly because for him it is the Moor. There is no metaphor. It is markedly different from Gloucester's feeling of despair in *King Lear*:

> As flies to wanton boys are we to the gods;
> They kill us for their sport. (IV.i.37–38)

Gloucester still believes in something, even a malevolent being is better than the nothingness Titus is fighting against. All is all gone. Titus laughs.

> Why, I have not another tear to shed.
> Besides, this sorrow is an enemy
> And would usurp upon my watery eyes
> And make them blind with tributary tears.
> Then which way shall I find Revenge's cave?
> For these two heads do seem to speak to me
> And threat me I shall never come to bliss
> Till all these mischiefs be returned again
> Even in their throats that hath committed them. (III.i.267–275)

He reacts with the clearest wish to revenge and shifts from passivity to activity. Lear, imprisoned with Cordelia, tells her his fantasy:

> When thou dost ask me blessing, I'll kneel down,
> And ask of thee forgiveness: so we'll live,

> And pray, and sing, and tell old tales, and laugh
> At gilded butterflies, and hear poor rogues
> Talk of court news ... (V.iii.10–14)

King Lear tells Cordelia of his wish. Titus instead expresses a bleaker fantasy:

> Come, take away. Lavinia, go with me;
> I'll to thy closet and go read with thee
> Sad stories chanced in the times of old.
> Come, boy, and go with me; thy sight is young,
> And thou shalt read when mine begin to dazzle. (III.ii.82–86)

Titus gave his sword to Saturninus in the first scene as a tribute to the Emperor. Now, in Act IV, Titus, ready to act, sends weapons to Chiron and Demetrius, of whose guilt he is now aware. With this he sends a quotation from Horace as an indictment of the murderers, which they cannot decipher. Aaron alone is aware that Titus knows their secret crimes.

Like Hamlet, Titus is a madman who pretends to be mad. Act V begins with Tamora disguised as Revenge, and her sons disguised as Rape and Murder, coming to both torment mad Titus and to manipulate him. They want him to bring Lucius back from the Goths. Here we see Titus feigning madness in order to complete his plans for revenge. Tamora says to her sons:

> This closing with him fits his lunacy.
> Whate'er I forge to feed his brain-sick fits
> Do you uphold and maintain in your speeches,
> For now he firmly takes me for Revenge,
> And, being credulous in this mad thought,
> I'll make him send for Lucius ... (V.ii.70–75)

This masque-like performance feels artificially contrived; however, Titus seems convinced. Titus asks her to:

> Do me some service ere I come to thee.
> Lo, by thy side where Rape and Murder stands;
> Now give some surance that thou art Revenge:
> Stab them or tear them on thy chariot-wheels,

> And then I'll come and be thy waggoner,
> And whirl along with thee about the globe. (V.ii.44–49)

Tamora is fooled by Titus' feigned madness and leaves her sons behind.

Titus captures them as easily as he killed Mutius, telling them of his plan:

> You know your mother means to feast with me,
> And calls herself Revenge and thinks me mad.
> Hark, villains! I will grind your bones to dust,
> And with your blood and it I'll make a paste,
> And of the paste a coffin I will rear,
> And make two pasties of your shameful heads,
> And bid that strumpet, your unhallow'd dam,
> Like to the earth swallow her own increase. (V.ii.184–191)

During the banquet he explains to Tamora as she eats:

> Why, there they are, both baked in that pie,
> Whereof their mother daintily hath fed,
> Eating the flesh that she herself hath bred. (V.iii.59–61)

Thus Titus projects the Gaia/Kronos/Saturn myth onto Tamora. He then is energised and restored.

He kills Lavina to end her suffering, finally kills Tamora, and as his work is complete he allows himself to be killed by Saturninus, who himself is slain.

Lucius orders a proper burial for his father and Lavinia, and also for Saturninus. Tamora, the "heinous tiger" (V.iii.194), however, is left to the natural world:

> But throw her forth to beasts and birds of prey:
> Her life was beast-like and devoid of pity,
> And being so, shall have like want of pity.
> (V.iii.197–199)

In her hunger she has eaten ravenously, and is now to be eaten. Aaron who has made a pact with Lucius to save his son is buried to his chest and starved. As he is dying, Aaron says:

> Tut, I have done a thousand dreadful things
> As willingly as one would kill a fly ... (V.i.141–142)

The Moor/fly reference here returns as if an inevitability. Lucius becomes the new emperor of Rome and order is restored.

In the paper "My contact with Josef Popper-Lynkeus", Sigmund Freud elaborated upon a metaphor that he first introduced in *Civilization and its Discontents*. Freud writes: "For our mind, that precious instrument by whose means we maintain ourselves in life, is no peacefully self-contained unity. It is rather to be compared with a modern State in which a mob, eager for enjoyment and destruction, has to be held down forcibly by a prudent superior class" (Freud, 1932c, p. 221). Each culture defines what is madness or what is psychotic and has an explanation as to its origins, whether star-crossed or sorcery.

While Freud was the first one who systematically explored the unconscious and interpreted psychosis as a breakthrough of unconscious processes, cultures before essentially knew that psychosis was indeed a breakthrough of unconscious processes, however the unconscious was defined in that society at that time. Even Aristotle in ancient Greece suggested that from birth man has a life that reflects the character he develops and the reactions he will have.

The doctrine of the Four Humours (sanguine, choleric, phlegmatic, and melancholic) derived principally from the writings of Galen (AD c.130–c.200), and, with the exception of Paracelsus, was widely accepted by medical men and scientists. The humours were used to explain man's physical characteristics and psychological "complexion". Each humour could become sick, a situation thought particularly serious in the choleric or melancholic humours, which were believed to produce different forms of madness. Moreover, a person's humour could also change under pressures from within; an excess of blood, yellow bile, phlegm, or black bile could all be altered from external pressures. In *The Anatomy of Melancholy* written in 1621, Robert Burton described the humours as either innate or acquired (Burton, 1621, p. 398). The question of innate or acquired, and of within or from without, still plague the study of psychology 500 years later.

Writing between Galen and Burton, Shakespeare refers little to the humours, while his contemporaries did this quite freely. While Shakespeare may have inherited the view of personality and medieval humours, he uses them only metaphorically, and expresses, instead, more dynamic aspects and the conflictual natures of psychotic processes. Shakespeare suggested a more complex working of the mind.

As Freud wrote that "Before the problem of the creative artist analysis must, alas, lay down its arms" (Freud, 1928b, p. 177), so too did Heinz Kohut say: "Art leads to psychoanalytic discoveries" (Kohut, Personal communication, 1974). It is in this spirit that we look to Shakespeare to teach us about the psyche. Madness in Shakespeare's plays is capable of being understood, and by this understanding becomes part of the human experience.

The Greek tragedies allowed a limited process of catharsis to unfold. In Shakespeare's plays something additional is enacted and identified with. If, as Freud wrote to Fleiss, "Each member of the audience was once, a germ and in phantasy, just such an Oedipus ..." (Freud, 1950a, p. 265) we are all budding Oedipuses, in that we identify with Oedipus, but are not privy to what he thinks and feels.

Oedipus acts. Macbeth thinks and feels. Thus action shifts to an internal process. The focus is not on inactivity, but on the internal world.

We identify with sad Hamlet, the ambitious Macbeth—even with his wife who pushes Macbeth to act out what she cannot. However, when Banquo's ghost appears we witness the breakthrough of the psychotic. We all are Lears. A career soldier during peacetime may be as uncomfortable as Titus is. Once we identify with these characters we are at the mercy of the dramatist.

Shakespeare willingly or unwilling draws us into empathy with madness.

It is interesting to note that for Shakespeare madness is the death of the self, and death of the body soon follows.

This madness is in stark contrast to the madness of Lady Macbeth or that of Ophelia; this stage madness picked up again by the Pre-Raphaelites, who held a more romantic view of madness and death. Their mad scenes are short and quotable, but stir little affect in the audience, as these two women speak their soliloquies as if in a trance. We do not feel their suffering, we only can see it with our eyes.

Regression is so profound in Titus as he is already a filicide. He led his sons to death on the battlefield in a way that he could rationalise and defend against knowing in a conscious way. When Titus is in the court and he murders Mutius he is really committing an act he has been doing all along, yet this time the defences fail him.

Great art can expand our views of psychoanalysis. Titus will never walk into our consulting room requesting an analysis. He organised his self from madness. He was able to do better than simply discern reality. He was able to observe the unconscious of others and was aware of the needs he had to accomplish his aim of revenge.

We may see aspects of Titus in psychosis and even aspects of Titus in terms of narcissistic vulnerably and one's attempt to restore self-worth—that is, to restore the fragmentation of the self, which is Kohut's elaboration of Freud's concept that slights which lead to regression proper may be restored through fantasy, even fantasy of revenge.

CHAPTER SIX

The future of an illusionist

The Tempest, William Shakespeare's final solo work, is one of his most popular plays. It continues to inspire artists of every genre. It is almost the shortest play, and critics often comment on its symmetry. The play begins with a shipwreck and magical arrival and ends with a ship restored and a magical departure. There is also symmetry in the themes: serenity and turmoil, legitimacy and usurpation, fertility and bareness, masculinity and femininity, and mature *vs.* adolescent drives. The entire play in form and content is a mirror image of itself. There are frequent interruptions in the speeches and in the actions. Even the language itself is especially abbreviated, and is so truncated that even the syllables collapse on themselves (Vaughan & Vaughan, 1999, pp. 14–21).

Like the classic epics of Greece and Rome, we enter during the storm in media res, not simply in the middle of the story, but as if we are interrupting something already underway. *The Tempest*, then, is a phenomenon that can be witnessed, but there is also an internal storm that rages and must be inferred from the text.

This play rigidly adheres to the unity of real time, more so than even *Julius Caesar*. Here the action occurs during the actual hours upon the stage.

We are on the deck of a ship, our holding environment (Winnicott, 1965, pp. 1–276), which is fragmenting on an unruly sea. We learn the King of Naples and his court are onboard as well as the Duke of Milan. The play begins by reminding us of the veneration for the monarchy. Gonzalo says, "Good, yet remember whom thou hast aboard." To which the boatswain replies "None that I more love than myself" (I.i.19–20). Sebastian, furious at the boatswain's irreverence to the Duke and to the King, exclaims: "A pox o' your throat, you bawling, blasphemous, incharitable dog" (I.i.39–40). The sea usurps the boat and leads it into Prospero's new make shift dukedom.

We now see the ship from the perspective of Prospero and Miranda on the enchanted island. We are in the realm of a magic land that can confuse the senses of its visitors. Shakespearean scholars seem desperate to locate this island on a cartographer's map; it is somewhere between Naples and Tunis, yet they attempt to travel to the exotic locales of Bermuda, the New World, Africa, or even Ireland. The audience never sees the Italian courts. Isolated geographically, the island is almost deserted with no true natives. It is as if, perhaps, we ourselves are desperate to escape.

Miranda is concerned for the people aboard, and although she idealises her father she knows that he is also capable of malevolence: "If by your art, my dearest father, you have/Put the wild waters in the roar, allay them" (I.ii.1–2). She continues:

> Had I been any god of power, I would
> Have sunk the sea within the earth or ere
> It should the good ship so have swallow'd and
> The fraughting souls within her. (I.ii.10–13)

Prospero attempts to reassure her that no one will be hurt and says: "No harm! I have done nothing but in care of thee …" (I.ii.15–16). It is not clear if this is true.

His need to restore his sense of self seems to eclipse all. One might wonder, moreover, if the false nature of the storm reflects the operation of a false self, a defensive structure that protects him and others from experiencing the full pitch of his rage (Winnicott, 1960, pp. 140–152). Prospero and Miranda appear to be afraid of the true tempest that his anger could unleash if left unchecked.

Prospero then goes on to reveal the story of their exile on the island. As he begins his tale he removes his magician's robes:

> 'Tis time
> I should inform thee farther. Lend thy hand
> And pluck my magic garment from me. (I.ii.22–24)

Thus he is returning to Prospero, without the costume of Duke or of magician. In finding the island, Prospero hoped to be different from his former self.

He insists that Miranda listen with great attention. Miranda responds that she is, saying:

> You have often
> Begun to tell me what I am, but stopp'd
> And left me to a bootless inquisition,
> Concluding, 'Stay, not yet'. (I.ii.33–36)

Something in him interferes with the telling of the tale. Miranda demonstrates that she is aware of his procrastinations. Prospero now asks Miranda what she remembers—not about her, but rather about who he was:

> Canst thou remember
> A time before we came unto this cell?
> I do not think thou canst, for then thou wast not
> Out three years old. (I.ii.38–41)

He continues his questioning with an increased urgency:

> By what? By any other house or person?
> Of any thing the image, tell me, that
> Hath kept with thy remembrance. (I.ii.42–44)

Prospero has a need to hold on to his own memories, as no one else on the island is witness to his past. The fantasy of revenge allows him some limited organisation. Prospero has returned all the actors in his earlier drama to this island. He plans to return the slights he has suffered onto those who have wronged him concretely—in exactly the same manner.

While Miranda does not remember her mother, she does reveal her earliest memory:

> Had I not
> Four or five women once, that tended me? (I.ii.46–47)

As a screen memory, the earliest memories reflect not only the past, but also the present (Freud, 1899a, pp. 303–322). We would read it that Miranda, by remembering that she was cared for, needs care in the present. Prospero, like a psychoanalyst, asks:

> But how is it
> That this lives in thy mind? What seest thou else
> In the dark backward and abysm of time? (I.ii.49–51)

Prospero needs her to remember the exile so that he has a witness of his past in his daughter, but she cannot:

> Twelve year since, Miranda, twelve year since,
> Thy father was the Duke of Milan and
> A prince of power. (I.ii.55–57)

Miranda asks:

> O, the heavens!
> What foul play had we that we came from thence?
> Or blessed was't we did? (I.ii.63–65)

She raises the question of whether it is good or bad to be on the island, to which Prospero responds:

> Both, both, my girl.
> By foul play, as thou say'st, were we heaved thence,
> But blessedly holp hither. (I.ii.66–68)

For Prospero it was indeed both; the exile and his disavowed contribution to it almost destroyed him, yet the island allows him magic to re-work and work through the rupture to his sense of self. Miranda now presses him for more information. Prospero describes his brother Antonio:

> he, whom next thyself
> Of all the world I loved, and to him put
> The manage of my state … (I.ii.74–76)

Prospero's syntax becomes jumbled and he omits words, attesting to his uncertainty and the rawness of feelings. His agitation is increasing as he speaks:

> … as at that time
> Through all the signories it was the first,
> And Prospero the prime Duke, being so reputed
> In dignity, and for the liberal arts
> Without a parallel; those being all my study,
> The government I cast upon my brother
> And to my state grew stranger, being transported
> And rapt in secret studies, thy false uncle … (I.ii.76–83)

He recognises he grew stranger to his state but rationalises that his studies were more important. Prospero continues:

> Being once perfected how to grant suits,
> How to deny them, who to advance and who
> To trash for over-topping, new created
> The creatures that were mine, I say, or changed 'em,
> Or else new form'd 'em, having both the key
> Of officer and office, set all hearts i'the state
> To what tune pleased his ear, that now he was
> The ivy which had hid my princely trunk
> And suck'd my verdure out on't. (I.ii.86–94)

He seems to be explaining how his brother was better suited as Duke, but quickly rationalises his own behaviour. He suddenly shouts again to Miranda: "Thou attend'st not!" (I.ii.94). Again, we have no reason to believe she is not listening. He questions Miranda: "Dost thou hear?" (I.ii.106). Clearly, what Prospero is describing is something painful to articulate. Antonio could not usurp the dukedom without Prospero's negligence and self-absorption, which Prospero has rationalised. He gives a good but false reason for his ambivalence in ruling Milan:

> Me, poor man, my library
> Was Dukedom large enough. (I.ii.109–110)

Prospero uses his books in distinct ways. When he was Duke, he used his books for knowledge; he also used them as an excuse to remove himself from the affairs of state. When Prospero and Miranda were exiled on the boat, Gonzalo had smuggled him these books:

> Knowing I loved my books, he furnish'd me
> From mine own library with volumes that
> I prize above my dukedom. (I.ii.166–168)

Prospero says "I prize"; it is in the present tense. Thus the books allow Prospero a touchstone to who he had been in Milan. On this enchanted island the books hold magical properties—which may reflect simply on the importance of identification (Freud, 1917e, pp. 237–258). Yet this magic allows Prospero limited self-knowledge, which results in power over others. The magic allows him to redo, reorder, repeat, and come to different conclusions about himself. As in life, this does not take place in a linear fashion, for he continues to make mistakes and his emotional life is dominated by the fantasy of revenge.

This man of action, well-loved as Duke, and with an audience as large as Milan, shifted to passively relinquishing his position and withdrawing. As for being Duke, he explains he was well-liked, yet he withdrew from the stage and into his studies. What happened immediately before Prospero retreated to his library in Milan? Was that the initial injury, rather than the banishment? Perhaps to restore Prospero to Milan is not the solution. Prospero easily blames his brother, yet it is Prospero's own struggle within himself that seems to cause his own undoing.

Miranda wants her question to be answered:

> And now I pray you, sir,
> First still 'tis beating in my mind, your reason
> For raising the sea-storm? (I.ii.175–177)

THE FUTURE OF AN ILLUSIONIST   143

She questions his motivations, a question he is unable to answer. His agitation suddenly becomes so great that he breaks off his narrative and magically sends her to sleep. Once again, as Miranda has noticed, Prospero cannot complete his story. Prospero, as magician, returns.

Whatever else Ariel can be to Prospero, he is not a witness. He is of the elements, and a figure in the revenge motif. To Ariel, Prospero is not the banished Duke, but a sorcerer. He is an alchemist who rules the natural world while attempting to maintain his dukedom and maintain power over human nature. Ariel is able to recall Prospero's magical powers but cannot be Prospero's witness to his time as Duke. Ariel begins by chiding Prospero much as Miranda did:

> Since thou dost give me pains,
> Let me remember thee what thou hast promised,
> Which is not yet perform'd me. (I.ii.242–244)

Instead of responding to the question of when he is to be set free, Prospero reminds Ariel of his history, and of Prospero's own great victory:

> Dost thou forget
> From what a torment I did free thee? (I.ii.250–251)

He chides Ariel for forgetting his liberation from the cloven pine:

> Thou liest, malignant thing! Hast thou forgot
> The foul witch Sycorax, who with age and envy
> Was grown into a hoop? Hast thou forgot her? (I.ii.256–258)

Prospero insists that Ariel recount all the details about Sycorax including where she came from, how she came to the island, how she imprisoned Ariel, and how Prospero freed him. Prospero reminds Ariel:

> What torment I did find thee in: thy groans
> Did make wolves howl and penetrate the breasts
> Of ever angry bears. (I.ii.287–289)

These words seem closer to the coloniser's insistence that he saved the savage indigenous people from their "unspeakable practices" and therefore the natives should be "grateful" to the imperialists who need their labour. This case is usually made about Caliban but is perhaps more suited to Ariel.

Transiently empowered by this reminder of his victory over Sycorax, Prospero orders Ariel:

> Go make thyself like a nymph o'the sea;
> Be subject to no sight but thine and mine, invisible …
> (I.ii.302–303)

Thus, throughout the play only Prospero can see him, and perhaps he exists only to Prospero. Ariel is a non-corporeal being who, unlike Prospero, has no need of memory; however, Prospero insists Ariel remember, restoring transiently his own sense of power. By ruling over Ariel, Prospero attempts to reorganise himself, and thereby learns to be a ruler as he never was in Milan.

Prospero also rules Caliban. While Ariel's memories are of imprisonment, Caliban's memories are of freedom. Prospero also rules Caliban and uses physical torments to keep him under control. He is not a noble savage as much as a savage vassal. Caliban enters with a list of grievances against Prospero:

> This island's mine by Sycorax, my mother,
> Which thou takest from me. When thou camest first
> Thou strokedst me and madest much of me; wouldst give me
> Water with berries in't, and teach me how
> To name the bigger light and how the less
> That burn by day and night. And then I loved thee
> And show'd thee all the qualities o'th' isle:
> The fresh springs, brine-pits, barren place and fertile.
> Cursed be I that did so! All the charms
> Of Sycorax—toads, beetles, bats—light on you!
> For I am all the subjects that you have,
> Which first was mine own king … (I.ii.332–43)

Caliban's relationship with the island is all that is left of his mother. With this and his experience with Prospero, the island, spoken of in idealised terms, may also represent a parental identification. Caliban is at times called a "moon-calf". This mythological creature, an infant born under the moon, is thought to be created solely by a female.

Caliban's wish for a father is not only for instruction but reflects his need for an identification. Caliban makes a case for himself as the true king of the island, but he is only a child and his fantasy of being king represents mere adolescent egotism and grandiosity. This is not dissimilar from Prospero, who believes that it was his brother's fault he could not rule Milan and does not recognise his own contribution to his own usurpation. Caliban was only twelve when Prospero arrived and could not have been his own king. Prospero did not know how to deal with Caliban, who seems to have no superego, much like Antonio. Prospero was unaware that Caliban, the very essence of earthiness, is ridden with unconscious drives and has neither conscience nor memory, except as he perverts it. Prospero says:

> In mine own cell, till thou didst seek to violate
> The honour of my child. (I.ii.348–349)

To which Caliban quite appropriately replies:

> Thou didst prevent me, I had peopled else
> This isle with Calibans. (I.ii.351–352)

Prospero, we postulate, suffering from these blows, needed time and objects to overcome the meaninglessness that plagued him. He uses all three characters on the island to this end: Ariel is used to fulfil his revenge and is controlled by memory of his imprisonment by Sycorax, Caliban is used for survival and is controlled by physical abuses, and Miranda, his "mirror" (in Latin), is used to recall his history and the misery he has experienced, rather than his power. However, this is not enough. Prospero, with an object hunger, needs the actual objects.

We meet Ferdinand, the son and heir of Alonso, the King of Milan, who unknowingly is one of the main actors in Prospero's revenge. Ariel has separated him from the others on the beach and convinces him through his song that his father is dead:

> Full fathom five thy father lies,
> Of his bones are coral made;
> Those are pearls that were his eyes,
> Nothing of him that doth fade

> But doth suffer a sea-change
> Into something rich and strange … (I.ii.397–402)

By convincing Ferdinand that his father has drowned, this song is reminiscent of the mock suicide of Gloucester in *King Lear*. Ferdinand is spared the full painful mourning process by immediately finding his lost love object in Miranda and a substitute father in Prospero. Miranda instantly falls in love with him. As the scene has been orchestrated by Prospero, with Ariel's assistance, he feels well on his way to revenge himself on Alonso. Prospero, however, slows the courtship:

> I must uneasy make, lest too light the winning
> Make the prize light. (I.ii.452–453)

Prospero is also denying his competition with Ferdinand. He uses magic metaphorically to control Ferdinand's sexual drives, and says as Ferdinand draws his sword:

> For I can here disarm thee with this stick
> And make thy weapon drop. (I.ii.473–474)

This comment can be heard as the fear of castration by the father or the father's desire to castrate the son, as in the primal horde (Freud, 1912–1913, pp. 1–161). Ferdinand, like the other sexual object Caliban, is made to be physically useful through stacking wood.

Gonzalo tries to soothe the King by playing on the amazement of their survival. Gonzalo is not who we expect; with Prospero's great gratitude towards him we expected him to be more Mark Antony than the Polonius that he proves to be. For Gonzalo praises Prospero's magic, or false self:

> That our garments being, as they were, drenched in the sea,
> hold notwithstanding their freshness and
> glosses, being rather new-dyed than stained with
> salt water. (II.i.63–66)

Alonso cannot be so easily comforted, for he is in mourning for his son. Adrian and Gonzalo wish to relieve the King. When Adrian speaks of the marriage of Claribel, the King's daughter, to the King of Tunis,

Gonzalo adds: "Not since widow Dido's time" (II.i.77) did Tunis have so great a queen. The multiple references to the historic Dido, the Queen of Carthage, who killed herself when left by Aeneas, contrasts starkly with Prospero. Aeneas left Dido when he went to fulfil his claim to re-establish Troy and Italy and to start a new culture; Aeneas was too encumbered by her and had to cast her off. Prospero, by contrast, has no Dido to hold him back and no ambition to find a new Troy.

Gonzalo describes an imaginary commonwealth made on the island: "And were the king on't, what would I do?" (II.i.146). He continues:

> I' the commonwealth I would by contraries
> Execute all things, for no kind of traffic
> Would I admit; no name of magistrate;
> Letters should not be known; riches, poverty
> And use of service, none; contract, succession,
> Bourn, bound of land, tilth, vineyard—none;
> No use of metal, corn, or wine, or oil;
> No occupation, all men idle, all;
> And women, too, but innocent and pure;
> No sovereignty ... (II.i.148–157)

This utopia is resurrected as an attempt to soothe the King, yet makes him more sorrowful for his losses. This is a magic island that stirs up man's ambition; even the drunken Stephano has plans to rule it. It is the potential anecdote to Prospero's disavowed abdication in ruling Milan; however, while Caliban, Gonzalo, Stephano and Ferdinand recognise the island as a potential new kingdom, Prospero does not. He cannot even rule his dukedom of three.

Ariel enters and puts the court to sleep, save Antonio and Sebastian. Here Antonio seduces Sebastian to kill his own brother while he sleeps. Antonio is to Sebastian similar to who Lady Macbeth is to Macbeth and who Cassius is to Brutus. Antonio says:

> They fell together all, as by consent;
> They dropp'd, as by a thunder-stroke. What might,
> Worthy Sebastian? O, what might?—No more;
> And yet, methinks I see it in thy face
> What thou shouldst be: the occasion speaks thee, and

> My strong imagination sees a crown
> Dropping upon thy head. (II.i.203–209)

He exaggerates the distance Claribel is from Naples.

> We all were sea-swallow'd, though some cast again,
> And by that destiny to perform an act
> Whereof what's past is prologue, what to come
> In yours and my discharge. (II.i.251–254)

Sebastian recalls: "I remember/You did supplant your brother Prospero" (II.i.272–273). Antonio responds:

> True:
> And look how well my garments sit upon me
> Much feater than before. My brother's servants
> Were then my fellows; now they are my men. (II.i.273–275)

"But, for your conscience?" (II.i.276) Sebastian asks. To which Antonio replies:

> Ay, sir, where lies that? If 'twere a kibe
> 'Twould put me to my slipper: but I feel not
> This deity in my bosom. (II.i.277–279)

These thoughts reveal that Antonio lacks a firmly established internal superego; moreover, it reveals his awareness that Sebastian also lacks an internal sense of morality (Freud, 1923b, pp. 12–66). It seems that Prospero's revenge on Antonio serves to expose him as a murderer. For his part, Sebastian is easily swayed.

> Draw thy sword: one stroke
> Shall free thee from the tribute which thou payest,
> And I the king shall love thee. (II.i.293–295)

As Antonio and Sebastian draw their swords to kill Alonso, Ariel awakens the King:

> My master through his art foresees the danger
> That you, his friend, are in; and sends me forth
> (For else his project dies) to keep them living. (II.i.298–300)

These lines suggest that Ariel does not know Prospero's full plan of revenge or he would not have called Alonso Prospero's friend. Yet we suspect that even Prospero does not yet know his own plans. Ariel acts for Prospero—that is, an action part of the banished, passive Duke.

The jester Trinculo and the drunken butler Stephano discover Caliban and they discover each other. Interestingly, the commoners speak in prose, while Caliban speaks in poetic metre. While Stephano and Trinculo call him "moon-calf", Caliban sees in them deliverance from Prospero's yoke. We travel from the troubled thoughts of loss, though to conspiracy, murder, the comic scene of discovery, and Caliban's hope for freedom—or at least a different master.

Meanwhile Prospero, unseen, observes Miranda and Ferdinand's courtship. Ferdinand tells Miranda that he is a prince and probably a king. They pledge their love and hope to be married. Prospero is content with this development, but is becoming impatient for revenge. He goes off to consult his books, leaving the audience with a sense of his disorganisation.

Caliban returns along with the butler and the jester. Ariel baits them by using their voices to insult each other. Stephano is furious after the barbs Ariel via Trinculo has thrown, and Caliban joins in with:

> Beat him enough; after a little time,
> I'll beat him too. (III.ii.83–84)

Caliban, to use Anna Freud's term, identifies with the aggressor, Stephano (Freud, 1946, pp. 117–131). Unlike Ariel, Caliban does not want freedom. He still needs a father and wants only to change masters. Yet to change he must first destroy his current master and thus hatches a plot to kill Prospero:

> ... I' th' afternoon to sleep. There thou mayst brain him,
> Having first seized his books, or with a log
> Batter his skull, or paunch him with a stake,
> Or cut his wezand with thy knife. (III.ii.88–91)

How Caliban enjoys the imagery of destroying Prospero. It is as if he shares Prospero's primitive superstition, as he too suggests that there is something special about the books and adds:

> Remember
> First to possess his books, for without them

> He's but a sot, as I am, nor hath not
> One spirit to command. They all do hate him … (III.ii.91–94)

Caliban assumes all creatures feel the same animosity and the same ambition as he does. Caliban then increases the rewards by offering Stephano a greater gift, Miranda. He thus tempts the butler as he himself was tempted, although now it seems Caliban has relinquished his libidinal strivings and offers the desire to Stephano:

> Ay, lord, she will become thy bed, I warrant,
> And bring thee forth brave brood. (III.ii.103–104)

Stephano needs no further convincing and says:

> Monster, I will kill this man. His daughter and I
> will be king and queen—save our graces!—and
> Trinculo and thyself shall be viceroys. (III.ii.105–107)

Again, we hear the island stir up others' ambitions previously unknown to themselves.

The aged Gonzalo is weary and needs to rest. Antonio reminds Sebastian of their plot and encourages him to try again when the King and his courtiers are sleeping. Prospero appears, invisible and silent, and spirits assemble a banquet. Sebastian, Antonio and Gonzalo react in their unique ways to the magic. Sebastian and Antonio, with entitlement, hurry to eat, while Gonzalo thinks of the spirits as inhabitants of the island, gentle and empathic without the artifice of more civilised people. As the court sits down to eat, Ariel appears like a harpy and says:

> You are three men of sin, whom destiny,
> That hath to instrument this lower world
> And what is in't, the never-surfeited sea
> Hath caused to belch up you, and on this island
> Where man doth inhabit you 'mongst men
> Being most unfit to live—I have made you mad … (III.iii.53–58)

This represents the only madness in Shakespeare that is not preceded by insomnia. Antonio and Sebastian draw their swords and Ariel continues: "Your swords are now too massy for your strengths/And will not be uplifted" (III.iii.67–68). Ariel names the crimes and the victim:

> ... that you three
> From Milan did supplant good Prospero,
> Exposed unto the sea, which hath requit it,
> Him and his innocent child; for which foul deed,
> The powers delaying, not forgetting, have
> Incensed the seas and shores—yea, all the creatures—
> Against your peace. (III.iii.69–75)

It is not that vengeance has been delayed but rather Prospero was unable to revenge earlier. The deeds have not been forgotten, and Prospero will have it that Alonso will experience the same sense of loss that Prospero had to endure:

> Thee of thy son, Alonso,
> They have bereft, and do pronounce by me
> Lingering perdition, worse than any death ... (III.iii.75–77)

The banquet disappears and Alonso, almost mad, goes off to seek his son, while Antonio and Sebastian bear their swords to kill one fiend at a time. Prospero, being satisfied that one portion of his revenge has been attained, returns to the lovers. He begins, for the first time, to appear softer and more accepting. He had been too severe in his punishment of Ferdinand. He tells Ferdinand:

> If I have too austerely punish'd you,
> Your compensation makes amends, for I
> Have given you here a third of mine own life,
> Or that for which I live, who once again
> I tender to thy hand. All thy vexations
> Were but my trials of thy love, and thou
> Hast strangely stood the test ... (IV.i.1–7)

Why does Prospero say a third rather than half his life? We think that his revenge took up the other third of his thoughts and feelings. Prospero cautions against pre-marital sex; however, he must have a legitimate heir to Naples. Here Shakespeare introduces a masque. Masques were performed in honour of royal marriages and seemed to have usurped the religious rituals of weddings. The plot, if we can call it one, was of disharmony and chaos giving way to harmony and joy. It was not meant to be replicable but rather a one-off extravaganza with dialogue, music, songs, and extraordinary feats of stagecraft. Perhaps during the Renaissance in England, the power of the church was not stable enough to evoke the seriousness of marriage and for political and social reasons the masque bestowed legitimacy on the union from not only God but the gods of old as well. In *The Tempest*, this tradition—for the first and only time—is preserved. Prospero begins the masque with the injunction: "No tongue! All eyes! Be silent!" (IV.i.59). Iris, the messenger of the gods, appears as soft music is heard, calling forth Ceres to come before Juno as she descends. Ceres, still pained by Pluto's kidnapping of Persephone, with the help of Venus and Eros, will not participate if they are invited. Iris reassures her that they will not appear. Juno then welcomes Ceres:

> Go with me
> To bless this twain, that they may prosperous be,
> And honour'd in their issue. (IV.i.103–105)

They sing together, using metaphors of earth's bounties. Ferdinand is amazed and asks Prospero if they are spirits. Prospero boasts:

> Spirits, which by mine art
> I have from their confines call'd to enact
> My present fancies. (IV.i.120–122)

This is similar to causing the shipwreck, which would also call characters to "enact" his "present fancies". Ferdinand is overwhelmed and says of Prospero: "So rare a wonder'd father and a wife/Makes this place Paradise" (IV.i.123–124) thus he appears to be under the island's spell. Ceres and Juno whisper, and call on Iris to bring the water nymphs to celebrate the marriage and join in the dance. Prospero speaks, disrupting the performance. In the ensuing confusion the spirits depart. The marriage masque marks the beginning of Miranda as a sexual woman. Yet this is an island devoid of women. These women are more striking for their absence: Prospero's wife, Claribel, and Sycorax. If this union, which Prospero states again and again, is part of his plan, and is actually his goal, then why does it not end with the soothing masque?

Finding rich and enchanted garments, Trinculo is the first to put them on. This echoes Prospero, for he had only dressed the part of Duke. Instead of a formal anti-masque into masque we are presented with masque into the grotesque; Caliban, Trinculo and Stephano are the costumed anti-masques, thus we go from order to chaos, reversing the purpose of the masque and leaving us disorganised. Once again Prospero begins a plot only to interrupt it. Prospero explains:

> I had forgot that foul conspiracy
> Of the beast Caliban and his confederates
> Against my life: the minute of their plot
> Is almost come. (IV.i.139–142)

Why is Caliban as big an enemy to Prospero as his own brother? Is this an example of the interchangeability of love objects? While not the first of the new genre of tragicomedy, the protagonist almost being destroyed by a comic character has surpassed this genre in its extremity. Ferdinand and Miranda are surprised by the intensity of Prospero's affects and she says: "Never till this day / Saw I him touch'd with anger so distemper'd" (IV.i.144–145). Prospero reassures Ferdinand, not Miranda, whom we know has seen her father in such moods before. In a monologue, Prospero reflects on life as illusion:

> … We are such stuff
> As dreams are made on, and our little life
> Is rounded with a sleep. Sir, I am vex'd;
> Bear with my weakness; my brain is troubled.
> Be not disturb'd with my infirmity. (IV.i.156–160)

Ariel apologises for not disturbing him during the masque, and adds that he was fearful of Prospero's anger if he did so.

Prospero and Ariel unleash dogs and hunters on the drunkards and the plotters run away with the pack in close pursuit. Prospero commands Ariel to:

> Let them be hunted soundly. At this hour
> Lie at my mercy all mine enemies.

> Shortly shall all my labours end, and thou
> Shalt have the air at freedom. For a little,
> Follow and do me service. (IV.i.262–266)

Ariel tells Prospero that the three culprits—the Duke, the King, and now Sebastian—are insane and the remainder are unable to assist them. Only Gonzalo is weeping at the plight of his superiors and Ariel suggests that if Prospero saw them: "… your affections/Would become tender" (V.i.18–19). Prospero reflects on Ariel's comment. Knowing that Ariel is air and without feelings, he muses that since he is, himself, human, he may surrender his anger; however, this acquiescence may also suggest that Prospero is so desperate for a mirror or approval that he will accept advice from even Ariel.

> The rarer action is
> In virtue than in vengeance. They being penitent,
> The sole drift of my purpose doth extend
> Not a frown further. (V.i.27–30)

We do not entirely believe Prospero. His speech is slowed with rambling sentences that are redundant, formal, distracted, and with little affect, which is proved during the incantation. It is derived from Ovid's poem of Medea (Ovid, 8 AD, pp. 190–191). Medea and Sycorax are our reminder, in this play, of destructive, primitive females from a very early mythology. Prospero's incantation ends:

> I'll break my staff,
> Bury it certain fathoms in the earth,
> And deeper than did ever plummet sound
> I'll drown my book. (V.i.54–57)

Prospero marks a circle on the ground and Ariel leads them all into it. Like a judge summoning up a case against Alonso, Sebastian, and Antonio, he pronounces his sentence on the guilty parties as Ariel sings. Prospero says: "I will discase me and myself present/As I was sometime Milan" (V.i.85–86). He changes his magician's clothes for his ducal robes. To Sebastian he is the devil. Alonso recognises him, and is consumed by the thought of his drowned son. Prospero is conciliatory, saying he, too, lost a child in the storm. Prospero then reveals Miranda and Ferdinand playing chess. Alonso is afraid to believe it and fears if

THE FUTURE OF AN ILLUSIONIST   155

he does he will lose his son again. Ferdinand convinces him that he is mortal. With each line contradicting itself, Prospero says:

> Welcome, my friends all!
> But you, my brace of lords, were I so minded,
> I here could pluck his highness' frown upon you
> And justify you traitors ... (V.i.125–128)

Prospero has not forgiven. Prospero, in his last lines, tells Antonio:

> For you, most wicked sir, whom to call brother
> Would even infect my mouth, I do forgive
> Thy rankest fault ... (V.i.130–132)

Gonzalo summarises:

> Was Milan thrust from Milan that his issue
> Should become kings of Naples? O, rejoice
> Beyond a common joy, and set it down
> With gold on lasting pillars: in one voyage
> Did Claribel her husband find at Tunis;
> And Ferdinand, her brother, found a wife
> Where he himself was lost; Prospero his dukedom
> In a poor isle; and of us ourselves,
> When no man was his own. (V.i.205–213)

They prepare to return to Naples. Prospero frees Ariel but not before asking him to assist the winds to bring the ship safely home.

Again Prospero's usurpation has been plotted and his murder planned.

> These three have robb'd me, and this demi-devil
> (For he's a bastard one) had plotted with them
> To take my life. (V.i.272–274)

For himself he says modestly:

> ... and so to Naples,
> Where I have hope to see the nuptial
> Of these our dear-beloved solemnized;

> And thence retire me to my Milan, where
> Every third thought shall be my grave. (V.i.308–312)

While more vengeance seems to be enacted upon Alonso than Antonio, it is Alonso who at long last offers Prospero that which he has so desperately been seeking. Alonso offers to be Prospero's audience and says to Prospero:

> I long
> To hear the story of your life, which must
> Take the ear strangely. (V.i.312–314)

In this strange epilogue, Prospero, like Puck in *A Midsummer Night's Dream*, directly addresses the audience. Prospero breaks the frame, the fourth wall of the theatre, and asks for applause, which would serve as the wind, he says, to take him to Naples, or if not, he will have to remain on his island, concluding with a couplet: "As you from crimes would pardon'd be,/Let your indulgence set me free" (Act 5, Scene 1, Epilogue).

At the play's end we feel it is unfinished; it is as if the actors have simply quit the stage. While the players begin in court, travel to nature, and return to court, we remained shipwrecked. We not only enter the play in medias res, it is also how it leaves us. Little happens, there is little action, and there is no journey. It is recounted, not experienced. There's no journey into nature; therefore, we are not surprised when we see little change in the nature of the characters.

The Tempest is considered to be the most revealing of Shakespeare himself and Prospero's retirement speech has often been likened to Shakespeare retiring from playwrighting. As we know Shakespeare was not only a playwright, but also an accomplished actor. Shakespeare himself is rumoured to have acted in 1598, in Ben Jonson's *Every Man in His Humour*, a play that had a character named Prospero. Although we cannot say with certainty that he acted the role of Prospero, and while we do not view art as psychobiography, perhaps *The Tempest* could be the retirement of one aspect of Shakespeare; Shakespeare the actor, who, like Prospero, performed for an audience.

When we examine *The Tempest* as psychoanalysts, it is evident that Prospero will be our primary subject—our analysand. He is complex, multifaceted, capable of erring, and capable of recognising his errors and attempting to correct them. We have previously described symptom formation from the point of view of manifest regression. Here we must elaborate on symptom formation as it refers to regression proper. Our reading follows Sigmund Freud's (Freud, 1913i, pp. 317–326) view of symptom formation, in which an injury in the object world initiates a manifest regression in the form of fantasy formation. If this does not hold or "heal" the wound, then regression proper occurs. In this stage oedipal and pre-oedipal objects are re-cathected. If our personal histories are pleasurable enough we can return to normalcy after a short time. If not, we become lost in the sense of meaninglessness and experience the "Weltuntergang" (world destruction) phenomenon, which is almost unbearable; words and symbols lose their meanings and we are in a black sea of emptiness (Loewald, 1979, p. 751). Sometimes it is time and a nourishing environment that keeps us physically alive and permits us to return to our pre-morbid self. At other times, false beliefs, delusions and peculiar bodily sensations become organised in a very peculiar self that may be observed in the psychoses.

We attempted to follow Prospero as he experiences the variety of these stages. Since we do not have a real patient who can correct us when we are wrong, we use the text to inform us. The major blow to Prospero has occurred twelve years before the time of the play—that is, his shame and humiliation that he was unable to rule. We suppose that this blow was so profound for his sense of self that it influenced all his further actions. In his regression he holds on to the benevolent father figure in Gonzalo, who gave him his books and other paraphernalia, which were so valuable to him in his reorganisation of self in the play. This action of Gonzalo's, often viewed as "the wisdom of the aged", is that which keeps Prospero from suicide. It is not enough, however, to bring him back to sanity. For Prospero is mad—a psychotic wracked with a sense of revenge; at times having difficulty finding objects to blame for his predicament. Time and a somewhat neutral environment have allowed his outbursts to be infrequent so that he appears calm and rational. The three delusional aspects appear in the form of an airy being, Ariel; a crude, uneducated and libidinal Caliban; and a naive, feminine aspect of himself in Miranda. His job is to control these diverse tendencies into a somewhat organised self. How can he free Ariel or Caliban or even Miranda without losing a cherished and valuable part? Shakespeare attempts to concretise these parts of self as others, but he is only partially successful. Miranda is the most real, followed by Caliban, but Ariel is the most unreal. Ariel, like some symptoms of primary process thinking, is the most difficult for Prospero to relinquish. The play is, in our opinion, an enactment of internal historic struggles, and presents us with the characters who figured in the original blow; Prospero's brother and the King of Naples. While we are pushing our thesis of the mad Prospero a little far, we are not divorcing it from everyday experiences which can resonate with all thoughtful audiences. Narcissistic slights are common to us all. They are especially observed in various transitions of life. The vulnerabilities of childhood are well-known, but they are also present in the emotional state we call love; in our choice of work; in midlife; and during the aging process. Notably, Peter Hildebrand used this perspective when he spoke about magical mastery of aging and *The Tempest* (Hildebrand. Personal communications, 1986). Prospero, by our own calculations, is no more than thirty-five to forty years of age and is quite close to Shakespeare by modern standards, as Shakespeare was forty-seven when he wrote *The Tempest*. Having been born to it, rather than choosing it, the profession of Dukedom was thrust upon Prospero because of his heritage. He created a myth for himself as a bookish Duke—a reader not a leader—sustained even in exile. James I was viewed exactly in this way and was threatened with expulsion during the early years of his reign. Miranda, quite rightly, accepted Prospero's inability to tell his narrative because the retelling of it caused great pain, the past being at such distance from current reality. It is only when Prospero reorganises himself in the form of a vengeful being that he is able to complete a greater part of his story but needs to break it off in the emotion of the recall. The revenge is centred on the others to experience the suffering he endured at their hands. Alonso must feel the loss of all he values—his children. Antonio, exposed for inciting Sebastian to fratricide, must be expelled from his position as Duke, which he had chosen for himself. Sebastian must experience the murderousness, which he had long kept repressed, and recognise that aggression is a part of him. We have commented on this phenomenon of revenge as an organising defence in *Titus Andronicus*.

To have witnesses who corroborate our narrative of self is important. As people age, and their family and friends die off, the mourning for such losses is easily understandable. What is frequently omitted is that losing old objects is the relinquishing of one's own past and this void can serve as a slight, producing depression and a sense of meaninglessness, in a neurosis or a psychosis. With such people, the retelling of their history, unlike Prospero's unsuccessful attempts with Miranda, helps in revivifying past memories, and, with a benign listener, helps to enliven the personality. At the end of such treatment, the past becomes better organised, and although not altogether corresponding to the events that sustained the previous self, one is sufficiently resilient to make for a somewhat cohesive self. Memory, organised in this way, may also help in the recall of other less-remembered events that will come to the surface in the process. Heinz Kohut (Kohut, 1971, pp. 205–264) described the mirroring and the grandiose transferences, which, if not attacked, can be helpful in reorganising the self. Kohut's work is helpful in illuminating the complex events that make a reordering of the past a necessity for further development. Aesthetics and culture, as well as certain cathected things, serve as D. W. Winnicott's (Winnicott, 1971, pp. 40–41) "potential space" between the self and the other, which is not always in the sphere of consciousness.

We seem to have moved a great distance from *The Tempest* to the metapsychological. Our aim has been to illuminate an aspect of the play that can easily be overlooked. We do not intend to reduce the play to pathological states. We do, however, hope to show that pathology and normalcy are not polarities. Both can enlighten those aspects that compose the human experience.

CHAPTER SEVEN

What Shakespeare teaches us about aging parents and their adult children in *King Lear*

One imagines that audience response to William Shakespeare's plays is a static phenomenon. Reactions to directing and staging notwithstanding, we assume the content more or less affects us as it did previous generations. The history of audience response to *King Lear* is surprising. Written in 1605, the play has only been performed as we know it since the nineteenth century. The play was thought to be intolerable as it was written. In 1681, after the restoration of Charles II to the throne and the lifting of the ban on theatres, Nahum Tate, an Irish poet, rewrote the play. In his version, Cordelia defeats her sisters and returns Lear to the throne, thus achieving a happy ending. Although *King Lear* technically is an easy play to stage, requiring little by way of scenery, it was thought "un-actable" (Foakes, 1997, p. 1). It is unlikely that the stark story alone would have turned Georgian and Victorian audiences away from *King Lear*. They enjoyed *Macbeth* and *The Tragedy of King Richard III*, both of which are extremely bloody, and include graphic murders of children. Perhaps there is something in the structure itself of Shakespeare's other dramas that somehow relieved the audience in a way that *King Lear* does not. For instance, *Othello* and *Hamlet* follow Aristotelian tragedy. In these plays the leading figure has a tragic flaw in their character that directly leads them to ruin. It is not only Iago's cunning, but also Othello's own jealousy that undoes him. Without Othello's flaw there would be no tragedy, and, therefore, some reassuring sense of inevitability may emerge. In attempting to apply this Aristotelian model of tragedy to *King Lear* we find it comes up short. It is not Lear's tragic flaw that leads to the tragedy but rather something very different.

Shakespeare's *King Lear* became increasingly popular after World War I, and even more so after World War II. It would seem something about this play is made palatable in times of great social disruption. It is as if the audience now knows what terrible forces can be unleashed in wars, and are therefore able to view the destruction in *King Lear* as inevitable and cathartic. It is only in the twentieth century that *King Lear* has reached the status of great tragedy.

We will explore the relationships between aged parents and their adult children and what we believe made this play intolerable for almost two hundred years.

The story of *King Lear*, in itself, is simple. Lear, at more than eighty years of age, has grown tired of the affairs of state. He divides his kingdom into three—one part for each daughter, and plans to live out his days in their care. He stages a so-called love test during which he will offer the choicest piece of land to the daughter who loves him most. While Goneril and Regan dramatically flatter him, Cordelia refuses to answer him, saying simply to herself, "What shall Cordelia speak? Love, and be silent" (I.i.62). Enraged, Lear banishes her, yet he soon finds that his remaining daughters not only will not care for him, but actively seek to destroy him. They dismiss his train of knights. During a great storm Lear becomes aware of the "beastliness" of human beings, and goes mad. Cordelia returns from her banishment with the French army and wages war on her two sisters in an attempt to return her father to the throne, but her army is quickly defeated. Cordelia and Lear are then reconciled as captives. She is condemned and later pardoned, but the pardon comes too late and Cordelia is hanged. Lamenting over her corpse, Lear dies of a broken heart.

Within the play there is the story of the Earl of Gloucester and his sons, functioning as a parallel narrative to Lear's relationship with his daughters. Gloucester's younger son, Edmund, born out of wedlock, plots vengeance against his father for his lot in life. Edmund convinces his father that it is not he but rather the "legitimate" son Edgar who is plotting to overthrow him. Edgar, hearing that his father is displeased, banishes himself from the court. Edmund betrays his father and accuses him of treason. For this allegation Gloucester is blinded and exiled, where he then meets Edgar, who is in disguise. Edmund meanwhile seduces Lear's two older daughters, and their ensuing jealousy results in their murder and suicide. Edgar kills Edmund and reveals his true identity to his father whose heart then "bursts" with joy.

The historical Lear was a legendary king thought to have ruled in the eighth century B.C.E. in a period between the Greco-Roman gods and Judeo-Christianity. The earliest recorded story of King Lear appeared in literature in 1135. *The Historia Regum Britanniae*, by the monk Geoffrey of Monmouth, describes the love test that King "Leir" uses to find husbands for his daughters, after which Leir's daughters "Gonorilla" and "Regau" whittle away Leir's followers from sixty down to one:

> But she, not forgetting her resentment, swore by the gods
> he should not stay with her unless he would dismiss his retinue, and be
> contented with the attendance of one man; and with bitter reproaches she told him how ill his desire of vain-glorious pomp
> suited his age and poverty. (Monmouth, 1135, p. 117)

This event is central to our understanding of Shakespeare's *King Lear*. Shakespeare often used *Holinshed's Chronicles of England, Scotland and Ireland*, first published in 1577, as a source for his history plays. The *Chronicles* is based, however, primarily on Monmouth's book. Shakespeare chose the story of the Earl of Gloucester from Sir Philip Sydney's *The Countess of Pembroke's Arcadia*. Sydney discusses the responsibilities of kings and the evils of rebellion. Sydney tells of the Edgar/Edmund rivalry as well as the blinding of their father, after which the brothers are strangely reunited (Sydney, 1590, pp. 219–221).

Shakespeare also borrows the trope of the fierce storm from this story. Edmund Spenser explains in *The Faerie Queene* that King Leyr divides his kingdom because he has no male heir. It includes the love test in which Cordelia says she loves Leyr "as behoov'd" (Spenser, 1590, p. 215) according to her bond. Spenser's Cordelia was also exiled, after which Spenser describes the reaction of his other daughters:

> But true it is, that when the oyle is spent,
> The light goes out, and weeke is throwne away;
> So when he had resigned his regiment,

> His daughter gan despise his drouping day,
> And wearie waxe of his continuall stay. (Spenser, 1590, p. 216)

From Spenser, Shakespeare adopts the idea that after the King resigns his kingdom his daughters could then allow themselves to "despise" him. In 1594 a play by an unknown author was performed in London called *The True Chronicle History of King Leir*. Shakespeare was clearly familiar with the script and it is postulated that he himself acted in it. In this play King Leir begins:

> Thus, to our grief, the obsequies perform'd
> Of our too late deceas'd and dearest queen ... (Stern, 2002, p. 3)

He thus explains that he is in mourning for his wife and takes the advice offered by his counsellors to retire. Despite the happy ending there are many similarities between this earlier play and Shakespeare's *King Lear*. What we find significant is how Shakespeare deviated from that text. Shakespeare telescopes the first seven scenes into one. He further excludes any mention of the Queen, and Shakespeare's Lear retires, not due to mourning but because he has grown weary of ruling. This will prove an important distinction.

King Lear is set in the distant past, far away from everyday life. We understand that Lear has had a long, peaceful reign. Gloucester too had long been a wise counsellor. What leads these intelligent and just men to folly? Is it just the foolishness of old men, as many critics suggest? Lear does succumb to the flowery prose and flattery heaped on him by Goneril and Regan. Gloucester similarly falls for the simple rhetoric and stratagem of his bastard son, Edmund. These faults of doting fathers seem minor, however, and not the hubris that leads one to great tragedy. Yet, we know that this play is a powerful drama; that it was deemed intolerable for generations, and that it must therefore touch upon some universal, deep-seated themes.

To explain the phenomenon among the aged of seeking dependence on their children, Therese Benedek postulated the concept of a loss of "energy" during the aging process (Benedek, 1952, p. 108). We would say, in less energetic terms, that the sense of self is crucial in aging, and the vulnerabilities to disruption must be constantly guarded or defended against. This is most true in the "old-old" (Tobin, 1999, p. 27) who suffer the disruptions of their historic self as colleagues, friends, and witnesses of their lives begin to disappear. Children are sources of narcissistic gratification, and reminders of the historic self. Therefore children are important as both an extension of oneself into the future and also as witnesses to one's past.

Freud, attempting to solve the theme of the three caskets in *The Merchant of Venice*, speaks of the love test in *King Lear*. He asks: "Is not this once more the scene of a choice between three women, of whom the youngest is the best, most excellent one?" (Freud, 1913f, p. 293). Freud then likens the triad to the three fates. Cordelia thus represents Atropos, the third sister who cuts the thread of life. He concludes that Lear, in rejecting Cordelia, is attempting to avoid his fate—that is, death (Freud, 1913f, pp. 291–301). Much can be said for Freud's mythic insights but Lear can also be viewed from other perspectives. It is our thought that something occurs between the aging parents and their adult children in this primordial atmosphere that allows a freeing of repressed aggression and sexuality to come to the fore. It is not the foolish choices of old men that bring about the tragedy. Rather it is the lifting of repression and the breakthrough of the drives that allows for the destruction of the characters, the court, and the society.

Some critics suggest that Lear is simply a selfish old man who engineers his own destruction by making foolish choices. Lear has been described as the "headstrong old man next door" (Wright & LaMar, 1957, p. xxxviii). Following this view, the love test is Lear's expectation of flattery, performed because of a character flaw. We tend to believe that the love test is more profound. Something happens in this scene that threatens his very sense of self. Lear describes his plans:

> … 'tis our fast intent
> To shake all cares and business from our age,
> Conferring them on younger strength, while we
> Unburthen'd crawl toward death. (I.i.38–41)

Lear is aware of changes in himself and feels the fatigue of ruling. He may even be aware of some changes in his capacities. He says he is afraid he is not in his "perfect mind". He would like to pass the affairs of state onto his daughters. In performing the love test, Lear asks:

> Which of you shall we say doth love us most?
> That we our largest bounty may extend
> Where nature doth with merit challenge … (I.i.52–54)

The assumption is that Lear has already made his division of the kingdom, saving the best part for Cordelia—his most beloved daughter. He knows which daughter will have the best piece, so why undertake a love test? At more than eighty years of age, he has a terrible need to hear his self-importance reflected back to him. Benedek emphasised that the aged parent needs the child to reassure him that he is still himself (Benedek, 1952, p. 110). When Lear asks: "Which of you shall we say doth love us most?" (I.i.52) he is doing more than inviting flattery—he is attempting to use the daughters' responses as a boon to his narcissism. Lear needs positive comments to feel worthwhile and to deny his aging and infirmities.

To the children, while forever beholden, the older generation represents a clear obstacle and they have to wait before they can acquire power, prestige, and leadership. To gain control of the kingdom, the two older sisters flatter Lear, as he requests. Goneril says she loves Lear:

> … Dearer than eye-sight, space, and liberty;
> Beyond what can be valued, rich or rare;
> No less than life … (I.i.58–60)

Regan, also using court poetry, says:

> … I profess
> myself an enemy to all other joys
> which the most precious square of sense possesses,
> and find I am alone felicitate
> in your dear highness' love. (I.i.76–80)

Both daughters supply Lear with a sense of his powerfulness. The vacuous flattery of his elder daughters is not the stuff that attacks his vulnerability, as authors such as A.C. Bradley propose (Bradley, 1986, pp. 51–52). It is instead Cordelia's inability or unwillingness to recognise Lear's needs that brings forth the torrent of his rage.

When it is Cordelia's turn she says nothing. Cordelia thinks about her love, "love and be silent" (I.i.65). It is as if she does not hear the question. Lear does not mean "Who loves me most?", or "Who can flatter best?" He asks, in effect, "Who can supply me with a sense of who I am despite the changes I feel in aging?" Cordelia will not give her father this that he desperately needs. When she answers "nothing" we presume she is attacking Lear; attacking who he was, and attacking who he hopes to still be.

Royalty may well represent the way a child, via transference, views his/her parents. In answering "nothing," Cordelia will not allow Lear to relinquish the omnipotent role he has for her. However, Lear does not want to abdicate the actual throne, he only wants to give away his land and the worries of state, while still maintaining his court and status. For example, he does not stop using the royal "We" until Act III.

Cordelia cannot acknowledge these changes occurring in her father. By refusing to participate in the love test she is saying that he is the same King Lear that he always was, rather than the king he no longer feels he is. And she also demands him to be a more potent sexual object than even he sees himself, as she immediately expresses her need to return Lear to the throne. During the love test Cordelia says to her sisters:

> … But yet, alas, stood I within his grace
> I would prefer him to a better place. (I.i.301–302)

It is not the hateful sisters but the "ideal" Cordelia and her insistence that Lear is unchanged from his younger self that leads the action of the play. Lear cannot live up to this ideal state once he has abandoned it. If Lear wants to outwit death by retiring from active life and only Cordelia opposes this, is she more moral than her sisters? She is more attached to Lear than they are, and she further maintains her virginal status, keeping her suitors at bay. Goneril and Regan, on the other hand, already have husbands, and will either have to live vicariously through their spouses or struggle to gain power themselves. Cordelia is aware that she must withdraw her cathexis from her father, yet is unable to do this. She explains:

> Why have my sisters husbands, if they say
> They love you all? Haply when I shall wed,
> That lord whose hand must take my plight shall carry
> Half my love with him—half my care and duty. (I.i.105–108)

However, Cordelia does not do this; when she marries the French king she uses his resources to wage war on Britain in an attempt to return Lear to the throne and in order to hold on to her idealised view of her father. Thus Cordelia interferes with Lear's autonomy under the guise of returning him to King. In the love test, Lear banishes Cordelia and will also banish the Earl of Kent for questioning his decisions. Kent speaks to Lear as if Lear were still king:

> Royal Lear
> Whom I have ever honour'd as my king,
> Loved as my father, as my master follow'd,
> As my great patron thought on in my prayers. (I.i.148–151)

Kent respects Lear in this scene and throughout the play protects him, representing the old ideal. Even Cordelia comments on his devotion:

> O thou good Kent, how shall I live and work
> To match thy goodness? My life will be too short,
> And every measure fail me. (IV.vii.1–3)

Kent sees Lear's love test as a foolish act of a wise man. Kent criticises Lear's banishment of Cordelia and says: "What wilt thou do, old man?" (I.i.155). Here he too is insisting that Lear maintain his former capacities which Lear may know he can no longer do. Kent, his faithful vassal, also attacks Lear by calling him "old man" and doubting his judgement, which Lear may suspect is already failing, and therefore Kent suffers the same fate as Cordelia. In this scene Lear must banish both Kent and Cordelia—or banish from his mind that which their comments represent. He cannot maintain their royal view of him and feels that therefore he is worthless, useless, and old. What Lear requires in the love test is twofold. Lear requires to be treated as if he were the same powerful object as in their childhood, and simultaneously treated as if he is aging, looking to his children to fulfil some aspects of his dependent needs.

The love test is thus really the question "Who am I?", and it becomes a leitmotif as the play proceeds. Lear asks:

> Doth any here know me? This is not Lear:
> Does Lear walk thus? speak thus? Where are his eye?
> Either his notion weakens, his discernings
> Are lethargied?—Ha! Waking? 'Tis not so.
> Who is it that can tell me who I am? (I.iv.222–226)

He asks his daughter's servant: "O you, sir, you, come you hither, sir. Who am I sir? (I.iv.77). Oswald replies: "My lady's father"

(I.iv.78). Lear's question of who he is began before the love test and becomes more desperate as the play continues. Lear tries to preserve what Federn described as the "ich-gefühl", the feeling of the self (Federn, 1932, p. 511). What we see in Lear is this attempt to preserve who he is.

In this play Shakespeare sets two aged fathers and their relationships to their adult children in motion. The love test is played out between Lear and his daughters and Gloucester and his sons. Gloucester begins the play explaining that he has two sons: Edgar by his wife, and Edmund by his mistress. He describes that Edmund had been out of court "nine years, and away he shall again" (I.i.33). Gloucester says he loves both sons equal:

> But I have a son, sir, by order of law, some year
> elder than this, who yet is no dearer in my account. (I.i.18–19)

The desire to send Edmund away again suggests that, despite what Gloucester says, Edmund's illegitimacy and presence in the court threatens the legitimacy of the court itself. Edmund plots to set up his brother, Edgar, presumably to take his inheritance. Edmund forges a letter and pretends to read it, hiding it suddenly when his father comes near. When Gloucester asks what he is reading, Edmund echoes Cordelia when replying to his father, "Nothing my lord …" (I.ii.32). Gloucester, unlike Lear, looks beyond the "nothing" and walks into Edmund's trap. The forged letter says:

> … maintain it to be fit, that, sons at perfect age
> and fathers declining, the father should be as
> ward to the son, and the son manage his revenue. (I.ii.72–74)

Why when beloved by his son is Gloucester so quick to believe that Edgar wishes to overthrow him? Edmund privately warns Edgar that his father wishes him dead and says:

> … I have told you what I have seen
> and heard—but faintly, nothing like the image
> and horror of it. Pray you, away. (I.ii.180–182)

This pantomime and parlour trick are enough proof for Edgar to leave the court and go into hiding. Again we notice how easily both the father and son are convinced of each other's guilt. Edmund tells their father that Edgar attempted to:

> Persuade me to the murder of your lordship,
> But that I told him the revenging gods
> 'Gainst parricides did all their thunders bend,
> Spoke, with how manifold and strong a bond
> The child was bound to the father. (II.i.44–48)

At this point Gloucester, like Lear, suddenly relinquishes his judgement and becomes dependent on Edgar. Initially, Gloucester sounds powerful, referring to Edgar as "abhorred villain" (I.ii.76) and "worse than brutish" (I.ii.77).

He asks Edmund about the letter, deferring to Edmund's judgement: "Think you so?" (I.ii.89), thus allowing his son to manage his affairs.

In *Moses and Monotheism* Freud suggests that in ancient times there existed a continuous murderous battle between the leader/father who kept all the women for himself and the young and growing sons who sought to overthrow him and take the women. It was only with the invention of morality—that is, religion, Freud postulated that this state of affairs ceased but continues to be represented in the unconscious of both parents and children (Freud, 1939a, pp. 7–137). In both situations Lear and Gloucester suddenly relinquish their judgement to their children. Shakespeare, in this drama, suggests that the parents must be both powerful and present so as to keep order. When the parents surrender some aspects of their power to their children, the children no longer can hold their forbidden hostile or sexual feelings in check. Fear alone is not enough to keep the society together. The presence of the actual object is necessary as well. We can postulate that when Lear gives away his kingdom before he dies he is in essence removing the repressive barrier of his children's destructive and sexual impulses. The fathers' abdication, then, is not only their own ruin but also represents the ruin of the society, a reversal of *Moses and Monotheism*.

The oldest parts of the legend of King Lear are the love test and the dissolution of his court of knights, which date back to the twelfth century. In exchange for his kingdom, Lear asks that his daughters care for him and his train of knights. This allows gratification of dependent desires and simultaneously allows Lear to maintain his powerful status as ruler of the knights; thus he is able to hold on to his identity as king and hold on to a stable sense of his historic self. Goneril and Regan interfere with Lear's autonomy under the guise of caring for him. Regan says:

> ... I look'd not for you yet, nor am provided
> For your fit welcome. Give ear, sir, to my sister;
> For those that mingle reason with your passion
> Must be content to think you are old, and so—
> But she knows what she does. (II.ii.421–425)

The sisters explain that they are rejecting his knights only because they are riotous. This has been described as the "purging of his soul of vanity" (Wright & LaMar, 1957, p. xxxviii). One hundred knights gives him a court, an army, and a sense of who he is, both to protect and to define him. Cutting back his army does not remove vanity, it destroys him, because Lear's train of knights is a concrete manifestation of his sense of self. The love test is the act of doubling each other's flattery. This doubling returns as the halving of affections in Goneril and Regan bargaining over Lear's knights. It is a foil to the love test; in the love test the sisters outdo each other on their description of their love for Lear, building up his sense of self-importance. Here they outdo each other in their destructiveness. As the number of his knights diminish, Lear says: "I gave you all" (II.iv.273), to which Regan responds: "And in good time you gave it" (II.iv.274). Lear says to Goneril:

> ... Thy fifty yet doth double five and twenty,
> And thou art twice her love. (II.iv.284–285)

Goneril says: "... what need you five and twenty, ten, or five ..." (II.iv.287). Regan says hauntingly: "What need one?" (II.iv.290). Lear's court of knights represent to him the arena in which he can enact the Lear of old while simultaneously being unburdened by his current deficits. Destroying this is a destruction of Lear himself. Lear begins his descent into madness. This madness is the fragmentation of the self. Lear's vulnerability and his need for objects to define him here become the source of this madness. Regan says:

> O, sir, you are old.
> Nature in you stands on the very verge

> Of her confine: you should be ruled and led
> By some discretion that discerns your state
> Better than you yourself. (II.iv.157–161)

Regan then dictates to Lear how to act, continuing:

> … Therefore I pray you
> That to our sister you do make return;
> Say you have wrong'd her, sir. (II.iv.160–162)

Cordelia is unaware of changes that are occurring in her father as he ages. It is only Goneril and Regan who are aware of these changes and they use this awareness to exploit him. They humiliate him for his neediness. First they cut away his train and then show him that he cannot even rule a small court of just himself. Lear responds:

> Ask her forgiveness?
> Do you but mark how this becomes the house:
> 'Dear daughter, I confess that I am old;
> Age is unnecessary: on my knees I beg
> That you'll vouchsafe me raiment, bed, and food'.
> (II.iv.163–167)

The self requires objects, be they selfobjects as Heinz Kohut has described (Kohut, 1971, pp. xiv–34) or love objects in a libidinal sense. When the daughters reject him and he loses them as objects he relies on his knights. It is only when these, too, are taken from him that there is the sense of the destruction of his internal world.

Gloucester's story is parallel to Lear's but it is not the same. When Edmund plots against him, Gloucester does not "go mad" but instead enters into the delusional system that Edmund has prepared. Gloucester says of Edgar:

> Our flesh and blood, my lord, is grown so vile, my lord,
> That it doth hate what gets it. (III.iv.141–142)

While Gloucester's role in the court is the wise counsellor and upholder of legitimacy and the laws—that is, the superego—his first appearance in the play, pointed out by Arnold Tobin, finds him retelling with gusto his sexual dalliance with a concubine and expressing joy in his bastard son (Tobin, 2002, personal communication). Gloucester says:

> ... though this knave came something saucily to the
> world before he was sent for, yet was his mother
> fair, there was good sport at his making ... (I.i.22–24)

Gloucester too readily seems to accept Edmund's view of Edgar as a potential parricide. Could it be that as he ages Gloucester is closer to the awareness of his own unresolved Oedipus, particularly as it relates to his legitimate heir? Edgar's role as an ideal son seems to increase Gloucester's distrust of him. Edgar and Cordelia are thus similar. Their "goodness" is threatening to these two old men who are "marching towards death".

We would postulate, then, that Gloucester protects himself from madness by externalising his impulses onto Edgar, using the following syllogism: "Edgar loves me as he is my heir. He wants me to die so he may inherit my fortune. He does not love me. He hates me and wants to kill me." In preliterate societies, one can observe the awe that age inspires. In such gerontologies the aged represent, by their closeness to the gods, great power. They are the protectors of the mores of the society—that is, the superego, and are also the bearers of the history of the group. In *King Lear* all these elements are attacked, partially by the sexual and aggressive impulses of the younger generation, and partially by the eagerness of the elders, Lear and Gloucester, to relinquish their roles as the awe-inspiring parents.

Unlike Lear, Gloucester, throughout most of the play, fails to recognise that the moral laws have been overthrown. While this protects him from madness, it opens him to Edmund's plotting:

> Go to; say you nothing. There is division betwixt the dukes, and
> a worse matter than that: I have
> received a letter this night—'tis dangerous to be spoken—I have
> locked the letter in my closet:
> these injuries the king now bears will be revenged home. There's
> part of power already footed; we must incline to the King.
> (III.iii.8–14)

Gloucester believes that feelings can be dangerous if spoken and relies on his allegiance to Lear for his own safety. Believing that the rules of society, including that of hospitality, still apply, Gloucester admonishes Cornwall, who has come to punish him, by saying: "Good my friends, consider/You are my guests" (III.vii.30) and again says: "I am your host" (III.vii.39). It is as if the law of conduct will keep the unconscious forces, which have already been unleashed, in check.

It is only Edgar, so much like Richard III, who can comment on his sense of his newly won omnipotence as he says:

> How light and portable my pain seems now,
> When that which makes me bend makes the King bow,
> He childed as I father'd! (III.vi. 105–107)

Shakespeare suggests that ambivalence in relationships between fathers and their children is universal, however he uses different characters to illustrate such phenomenon—that is, Cordelia *vs.* Goneril and Regan, and Edgar *vs.* Edmund. If we look closely, however, such distinctions are blurred. For example, Shakespeare chose the name Edgar, to represent Gloucester's good son, from King Edgar reigning from 959 to 975, who was known for his cruelty, and Edmund from the King of East Anglia, who reigned from 841 until his death and is remembered as a saint (Holinshed, 1577, pp. 694–696). While Edgar disguises himself as Tom o' Bedlam it is Edmund who first mentions Bedlam, saying of his brother:

> And pat he comes, like the catastrophe of the old
> comedy my cue is villainous melancholy, with a
> sigh like Tom o' Bedlam. (I.ii.134–136)

Here we see how interchangeable the siblings are as they share the same disguise. Is not Edgar as devious as Edmund while he continues to hide his identity from his blind father? Stanley Cavell generously suggests that Edgar does not reveal himself in an attempt to deny Gloucester's blindness, and keep him the powerful father of his youth (Cavell, 1987, p. 56). How similar is this to our earlier suggestion that Cordelia does much the same, as she burdens Lear with her unresolved oedipal issues. Edgar says: "Bless thy sweet eyes, they bleed" (IV.i.57) and offers to lead Gloucester, but remains hidden in his disguise although Gloucester pleads:

> O dear son Edgar
> The food of thy abused father's wrath!
> Might I but live to see thee in my touch,
> I'd say I had eyes again! (IV.i.23–26)

Here is a second chance for Gloucester, and at this junction his "good" son is in control. When Gloucester says "I'd say I had eyes again" if he were to meet Edgar, his son demurs and does not reveal himself. Edgar muses:

> Why I do trifle thus with his despair
> Is done to cure it. (IV.vi.33–34)

We suppose that an additional reason why Edgar trifles with his father's misery is an enactment of his own ambivalence towards his father. He is the alter ego of his brother. Edmund acts out the destructive impulse that the "good" Edgar is seemingly not conscious of. When Edgar pretends that they are at the cliff's edge and Gloucester jumps, we note the sadism of Gloucester's mock suicide. We do not think that Edgar is "purifying" his father, as some critics have suggested, but rather is expressing his own rageful impulses towards Gloucester.

In many ways, Gloucester represents the traditional tragic figure. He sets out on his journey to Dover, through which he gains understanding of the extent of his ruin, and wishes to end his life. An understanding of the extent of the destruction is something Lear does not achieve, even in his madness. Gloucester says:

> 'Twas yet some comfort
> When misery could beguile the tyrant's rage
> And frustrate his proud will. (IV.vi.60–62)

In the past, misery and suffering had meaning—and even power, but now Gloucester is aware that suffering is meaningless, as humanity and society have been lost. Lear refuses offers of protection and goes out into the tempest. The weather may represent a projection onto the environment of the negative aspects of the self, in an attempt to retain the positive aspects in his internal world. In this way he can use his active struggle with the external world to protect himself from what is occurring internally. The leitmotif of Lear's question, "Who am I?"

is teamed with Lear's examination of his external trappings. Until the late nineteenth century the role of King Lear was always performed wearing royal robes (Foakes, 1997, p. 12). Lear asks if he can undress. He says: "pray you, undo this button" (V.iii.65). A king is his clothes, as clothing defines one's person. For Lear in particular they represent some aspect of the self. Each attempt to undress is an attempt to undo himself, or to illustrate the sense that he has, and that his internal world is undone. Lear says:

> Unaccommodated man is no more but such a poor bare,
> forked animal as thou art. Off, off, you lendings!
> come unbutton here. (III.iv.105–107)

Lear explains that it is only cloth that distinguishes man from beast and asks: "Is man no more than this?" (III.iv.101). Much of the language of the play also relates to the reduction of men to beasts. This is achieved through the uses of animal sounds, and animal metaphors. Lear describes how his daughter:

> … struck me with her tongue,
> Most serpent-like, upon the very heart … (II.iv.172–173)

He describes his children as "pelican daughters" (III.iv.74), as it was believed that pelicans fed their offspring with their own blood (Foakes, 1997, p. 276). Lear also calls them "unnatural hags" (II.iv.305), "she-foxes" (III.vi.22), "centaurs" (IV.vi.138) and confuses them for little dogs that all bark at him (III.vi.63). Lear threatens Cordelia with cannibalism when he says:

> … he that makes his generation messes
> To gorge his appetite, shall to my bosom
> Be as well neighbour'd … (I.i.18–19)

Albany too evokes animalism and cannibalism as he says:

> Humanity must perforce prey on itself,
> Like monsters of the deep. (IV.ii.50–51)

While it has been suggested that these animal forces "fling themselves upon" defenceless human beings (Bradley, 1986, pp. 219–220), in *King Lear* it seems more likely that these many animal sounds and metaphors, as well as hints of cannibalism, serve to reveal the beast within man. Lear attempts to restore a sense of justice by holding a mock trial of his daughters.

Lear, addressing Edgar, says:

> … I will arraign them straight.
> Come, sit thou here, most learned justicer;
> Thou, sapient sir, sit here. (III.vi.20–22)

Using Edgar (as Tom o' Bedlam) and the Fool as fellow justices and authority, Lear puts an imaginary Goneril and Regan on trial in the hovel. Lear orders:

> Arraign her first, 'tis Goneril—I here take my
> oath before this honourable assembly, she kicked the
> poor king her father. (III.vi.46–48)

Of Regan, Lear says:

> And here's another whose warp'd looks proclaim
> What store her heart is made on. Stop her there!
> Arms, arms, sword, fire! Corruption in the place!
> False justicer, why hast thou let her 'scape? (III.vi.52–55)

Lear reasserts himself in his small court of Kent, the Fool and Tom o' Bedlam, thus transiently overcoming his regression. Lear attempts to restore a sense of order but it does not hold. We watch it give way as he interrupts the trial and exclaims:

> The little dogs and all, Tray, Blanch and
> Sweet-heart, see, they bark at me. (III.vi.60–61)

These three dogs represent his daughters' interference. He puts mankind on trial, and attempts to restore law to a society that has lost its morality.

In the storm Lear describes his objectless state and likens it to the destruction of the world.

> ... smite flat the thick rotundity o' the world!
> Crack nature's moulds, all germens spill at once
> That make ingrateful man! (III.ii.7–9)

Lear's metaphors are like the "Weltuntergang" phenomenon (Loewald, 1979, p. 751) during which one feels as if the world has been destroyed to understand feelings of an objectless state. As his internal world is destroyed all objects within it are decathected.

In the play's first scene, Kent stops Lear's prayers and says:

> Now by Apollo, King,
> Thou swear'st thy gods in vain. (I.i.161–162)

Only morality can separate the primitive from a sense of orderliness. The gods will not work because morality no longer works. In this play the gods are destroyed. There is a breakthrough of the primitive female deities with their ties to nature and at the same time the play is set on a sparse, barren landscape in which there are no mothers. When Lear curses Goneril he prays for her sterility. He says:

> Hear, Nature, hear, dear goddess, hear!
> Suspend thy purpose if thou didst intend
> To make this creature fruitful!
> Into her womb convey sterility!
> Dry up in her the organs of increase ... (I.iv.268–272)

This play, therefore, can also represent an end to generations. Gloucester says: "O, let me kiss that hand!" (IV.vi.127) to which Lear replies: "Let me wipe it first; it smells of mortality" (IV.vi.128).

At the end of the play both Kent and Edgar refuse the kingship; therefore there is no one available to become king, and to re-establish things as they were before. Edgar says:

> The weight of this sad time we must obey,
> Speak what we feel, not what we ought to say.

> The oldest hath borne most; we that are young
> Shall never see so much, nor live so long. (V.iii.322–325)

Edgar believes that he has been cleansed and that the destruction is over, but he is in error. Speaking what one feels and not what one is supposed to say is to repeat Cordelia's part in what began this tragedy. This reminds us that the struggle is constant and must be worked out between every generation.

Lear says to Cordelia as he imagines their time together in prison:

> We two alone will sing like bird i' the cage.
> When thou dost ask me blessing I'll kneel down
> And ask of thee forgiveness. So we'll live
> And pray, and sing, and tell old tales, and laugh
> At gilded butterflies, and hear poor rogues
> Talk of court news; and we'll talk with them too—
> Who loses and who wins; who's in, who's out;
> And take upon's the mystery of things
> As if we were God's spies. And we'll wear out
> In a wall'd prison packs and sects of great ones
> That ebb and flow by the moon. (V.iii.8–18)

Curiously enough, as a prisoner he has more of a court than with his soldiers. To be imprisoned with Cordelia is, for Lear, to get what he wanted from the love test; a witness of his historic self and someone who will care for him. This is the second time the love-test is attempted and the second time it fails. External reality prevents Lear from achieving what he needed from the love test. Cordelia is hanged. Lear dies, as there is no alternative. The real sense of tragedy in *King Lear*, and what made it intolerable to audiences, is not merely character flaws but something more profound. The tragedy is the sense of the breakthrough of powerful unconscious processes, with their unmodified aggression and primitive sexuality, which disrupts the fragile orderliness that we impose in our attempts to keep chaos at bay.

AFTERWORD

In this small volume we used our close reading of selected Shakespeare plays to teach us about the human condition. We examined characters while listening to the ideas of Klein, Winnicott, Kohut, and Freud. Instead of a traditional psychoanalytic reading we discovered something quite different. Whether it's the metapsychology of evil, positive aspects of revenge fantasy as restorative to the ego or self, glimpses of incomplete identification and anaclitic depression in an adult, or aging parents and their adult children. Our conclusions are not a re-statement of the above, but rather leave us with renewed vigour to encourage the reader to reread, re-engage, rethink, and re-experience one's relationship with these texts. Our reading is by no means a definitive interpretation, nor is it meant to be. We have simply attempted to illustrate our way of seeing. Furthermore we would caution against any definitive reading of any art, by either an individual or a society. To read a text, listen to music or view visual arts is not actually natural, easy, or teachable. While one may suggest this is perhaps due to a defence against reality, this is not the case.

Viewing art is a private and intensely personal relationship that takes great effort, yet offers a specific reward. Art actually opens the world for the individual, and through this process, changes us, and opens us to the world.

We are reminded of John Keats' "On First Looking into Chapman's Homer". The first half of the poem seems to reflect Keats' intellectual reaction to reading that which society deemed important. However, when he first reads Chapman's translation Keats no longer simply sees but feels.

It is our hope that you approach each piece of art in your own way and remain open to what it may teach you about not only the world, but also yourself.

REFERENCES

Adelman, J. (1992). *Suffocating Mothers: Fantasies of Maternal Origin in Shakespeare's Plays, Hamlet to The Tempest*. London: Routledge.
Alexander, F. (1921). *The Scope of Psychoanalysis. 1925–1961: Selected Papers*. New York: Basic Books, 1961.
Aristotle. (335 BCE). *Poetics*. R. Kross (Trans.), New York: Dover, 1997.
Auden, W. H. (1962). *The Dyer's Hand*. New York: Random House.
Benedek, T. (1952). Personality development. In: F. Alexander & H. Ross (Eds.), *Dynamic Psychiatry*. Chicago: University of Chicago.
Bloom, H. (1998). *Shakespeare: The Inventor of the Human*. New York: Riverhead.
Bollas, C. (1987). *The Shadow of the Object: Psychoanalysis of the Unthought Known*. New York: Columbia University.
Bradley, A. C. (1986). *Shakespearean Tragedy*. New York: Ballantine Books.
Breuer, J., & Freud, S. (1895d). *Studies on Hysteria*. J. Strachey & A. Freud (Eds.), J. Strachey (Trans.), New York: Basic Books, 2009.
Brown, J. R. (Ed.) (1955). *The Arden Shakespeare: The Merchant of Venice*. Surrey: Thomas Nelson, 1997.
Burton, R. (1621). *The Anatomy of Melancholy*. New York: NYRB Classic, 2001.
Cavell, S. (1987). *Disowning Knowledge in Six Plays of Shakespeare*. Cambridge: Cambridge University.

Coleridge, S. T. (1849). *Notes and Lectures upon Shakespeare and some of the Old Poets and Dramatists*. London: William Pickering.

Daniell, D. (Ed.) (1998). *The Arden Shakespeare: Julius Caesar*. London: Thompson.

Eliot, T. S. (1950). Seneca in Elizabethan translation. In: T. S. Eliot (Ed.), *Selected Essays 1917–1932*. New York: Harcourt, Brace & World.

Federn, P. (1932). Ego feeling in dreams. *The Psychoanalytic Quarterly, 1*: 511–542.

Foakes, R. A. (Ed.) (1997). *The Arden Shakespeare: King Lear*. London: Thomson.

Freud, A. (1936). *The Ego and the Mechanisms of Defense*. C. Baines (Trans.), New York: International Universities, 1946.

Freud, S. (1899a). Screen memories. *S. E., 3*: 301–322. London: Hogarth.

Freud, S. (1900a). *The Interpretation of Dreams. S. E., 4*: 264–266. London: Hogarth.

Freud, S. (1905d). *Three Essays on the Theory of Sexuality. S. E., 8*: 135–243. London: Hogarth.

Freud, S. (1910h). A special type of choice of object made by men. *S. E., 11*: 165–175. London: Hogarth.

Freud, S. (1912–1913). *Totem and Taboo. S. E., 13*: 1–161. London: Hogarth.

Freud, S. (1913f). Theme of the three caskets. *S. E., 12*: 291–301. London: Hogarth.

Freud, S. (1913i). The disposition to obsessional neurosis. *S. E., 12*: 317–326. London: Hogarth.

Freud, S. (1914c). On narcissism. *S. E., 14*: 67–102. London: Hogarth.

Freud, S. (1915e). The unconscious. *S. E., 14*: 161–215. London: Hogarth.

Freud, S. (1917e). Mourning and melancholia. *S. E., 14*: 243–258. London: Hogarth.

Freud, S. (1920g). *Beyond the Pleasure Principle. S. E., 18*: 7–61. London: Hogarth.

Freud, S. (1923b). *The Ego and the Id. S. E., 19*: 12–66. London: Hogarth.

Freud, S. (1928b). Dostoevsky and parricide. *S. E., 21*: 177. London: Hogarth.

Freud, S. (1932c). My contact with Josef Popper-Lynkeus. *S. E., 22*: 22. London: Hogarth.

Freud, S. (1939a). *Moses and Monotheism. S. E., 23*: 7–137. London: Hogarth.

Freud, S. (1942a). Psychopathic characters on the stage. *S. E., 7*: 246–309. London: Hogarth.

Freud, S. (1950a [1887–1902]). *Extracts from the Fliess Papers. S. E., 1*: 265. London: Hogarth.

Freud, S. (1950a [1887–1902]). *Project for a Scientific Psychology. S. E., 1*: 295–387. London: Hogarth.

Green, A. (1986). *On Private Madness*. London: Karnac, 1997.
Hazlitt, W. (1814). *Character of Shakespeare's Plays*. London: Taylor and Hessey, 1818.
Hildebrand, P. (1986). The British Psychoanalytic Society, London. Personal communications.
Holinshed, R. (1577). *Holinshed's Chronicles of England, Scotland, and Ireland*. London: J. Johnson, 1807.
Honigmann, E. A. J. (Ed.) (1997). *The Arden Shakespeare: Othello*. Surrey: Thomas Nelson and Sons.
Jacobus, M. (2005). *The Poetics of Psychoanalysis*. Oxford: Oxford University.
Johnson, S. (1864). *The Plays of William Shakespeare*. Edinburgh: W. P. Nimmo.
Jonson, B. (1641). *Ben Jonson's Timber or Discoveries*. R. S. Walker, (Ed.), New York: Syracuse University, 1953.
King, H. (1993). Once upon a text: Hysteria from Hippocrates. In: S. L. Gilman, H. King, R. Porter, G. S. Rousseau, & E. Showalter (Eds.), *Hysteria beyond Freud*. Berkeley, CA: University of California.
Klein, M., Heimann, P., Issacs, S., & Riviere, J., (Eds.) (1952). *Developments on Psycho-Analysis*. London: Hogarth.
Kohut, H. (1971). *The Analysis of the Self*. New York: International Universities.
Kohut, H. (1974). The Chicago Institute for Psychoanalysis, Chicago, IL. Personal communication.
Kohut, H. (1984). *How Does Analysis Cure?* A. Goldberg & P. E. Stepansky (Eds.), Chicago: University of Chicago.
Loewald, H. W. (1979). The waning of the Oedipus complex. *Journal of the American Psychoanalytic Association, 27*: 751–775.
Mahler, M. (1968). *On Human Symbiosis and the Vicissitudes of Individuation*. New York: International Universities.
Monmouth, G. (1135). Geoffrey of Monmouth's British History. In: J. A. Giles (Ed.), *Old English Chronicles*. London: George Bell & Sons, 1906.
Ovid. (8 AD). *Metamorphoses*. H. Gregory (Trans.), New York: Mentor, 1960.
Palmer, D. J. (1972). The unspeakable in pursuit of the uneatable: language and action in Titus Andronicus. *Critical Quarterly, 14*(4): 320–339.
Platter, T., & Williams, C. (1599). *Thomas Platter's Travels in England, 1599*. London: J. Cape, 1937.
Plutarch. (1579). *Plutarch's Lives of the Noble Grecians and Romans, Englished by Sir Thomas North in Ten Volumes*. Volume VII. London: J. M. Dent, 1910a.
Rosen, I. (2007). Revenge—the hate that dare not speak its name: A psychoanalytic perspective. *Journal of the American Psychoanalytic Association, 55*(2): 595–620.

Rothenberg, A. (1971). The oral rape fantasy and rejection of mother in the imagery of Shakespeare's Venus and Adonis. *Psychoanalytic Quarterly*, 40: 447–468.
Rustin, M., & Rustin, M. (2002). *Mirror to Nature: Drama, Psychoanalysis and Society*. London: Karnac.
Spenser, E. (1590). *The Faerie Queene*. P. C. Bayley (Ed.), Oxford: Oxford University, 1965.
Steiner, G. (1961). *The Death of Tragedy*. New York: Faber and Faber.
Stern, T. (Ed.) (2002). *The True Chronicle History of King Leir*. London: Nick Hern.
Sydney, P. (1590). *Sir Philip Sidney's Arcadia Moderniz'd By Mrs Stanley*. London, 1725.
Terman, D. (1984). The self and the Oedipus complex. *Annual of Psychoanalysis*, 12: 87–104.
Tobin, A. (2002). The Chicago Institute for Psychoanalysis, Chicago, IL. Personal communication.
Tobin, S. (1999). *Preservation of the Self in the Oldest Years*. New York: Springer.
Vaughan, V. M., & Vaughan, A. T. (Eds.) (1999). *The Arden Shakespeare: The Tempest*. London: Thomson.
Winnicott, D. W. (1958). Transitional objects and transitional phenomena. In: D. W. Winnicott (Ed.), *Collected Papers*. New York: Basic Books.
Winnicott, D. W. (1960). Ego distortions in terms of true and false self. In: D. W. Winnicott (1965). *The Maturational Processes and the Facilitating Environment*. New York: International Universities.
Winnicott, D. W. (1965). *The Maturational Processes and the Facilitating Environment*. London: Hogarth.
Winnicott, D. W. (1971). *Playing and Reality*. New York: Basic Books.
Wright, L. B., & LaMar, V. A. (Eds.) (1957). *The Folger Library General Reader's Shakespeare King Lear*. New York: Washington Square.

INDEX

Adelman, J. 18
Alexander, F. 80
Anatomy of Melancholy, The 133
Antipholus of Ephesus 19
Antonio (*The Merchant of Venice*) 52–61, 63–65, 69, 74, 80
Antonio (*The Tempest*) 141–142, 145, 147–148, 150–151, 154–156, 158
Antony 83–86, 91, 97, 102–112, 146
Antony and Cleopatra 84
Arabian Nights, The 96
Arthur (nephew of King John) 26–27
As You Like It 9, 26
Auden, W. H. 13, 18

Baptista Minola 26
Bassanio 54–65, 69, 80–81
Belmont 56–57, 59–60, 62, 64–65
Benedek, T. 164, 166
Bloom, H. 18, 36, 53, 112, 115

Bollas, C. 89
Bradley, A. C. 166, 177
Breuer, J. 126
Brown, J. R. 53–54, 62
Brutus 84, 86–93, 95–98, 100–113, 147
Burton, Robert 133

Caesar, Julius 14, 84–92, 94–113
Caska 92–95, 101
Cassio, Michael 4, 8–10, 13
Cassius, Caius 84, 86–98, 100–104, 107–111, 113, 147
Cavell, S. 174
Chronicles, The 163
Cicero 84, 91, 93–94, 96, 107
Cinthio, Giraldi 3
Civilization and its Discontents 133
Clarence 28–29, 31, 33
cold fire 78
Coleridge, S. T. 3
Comedy of Errors, The 18–20

INDEX

Coriolanus 22, 27, 41, 44, 84, 124
Coriolanus 44, 46–48, 119, 124
Countess of Pembroke's Arcadia, The 163
"crows to peck the eagles" (III.i.140) 46

Daniell, D. 107
Darwin, Charles 92
Desdemona 3–6, 8–14
"dogs of war, the" 83
"Dreams in Pairs and Series" 80
Duchess of York 30–33, 44, 48
Duke Frederick 26
Duke of Milan 26, 138
Duke Senior 26
Dunsinane Hill 24

Earl of Gloucester 162
ego 35
Eliot, T. S. 18, 115
Elizabethan audience 90, 101
Elizabethan character formation 124
Elizabethan drama 4, 51
"Et tu, Brute" 83
Every Man in His Humour 156

Faerie Queene, The 163
false self 87, 138, 146
father–daughter relationships 2, 25, 57–58, 60–63, 80, 82, 117, 119, 138, 140, 162, 164, 166–170, 172, 174, 177
  Juliet 68, 77, 80
father–son relationships 2, 18, 58, 90, 92, 109, 112–113, 116, 121, 127, 145–146, 149, 157, 162–164, 169–170, 174
  Hamlet 35–36, 43–44
  Romeo 67
feather of lead 78
Federn, P. 169

Ferdinand 145–147, 149, 151–155
feudal society 81
Fiorentino, Giovanni 54
Foakes, R. A. 161, 176
Forest of Arden 26, 56
Freud, A. 88, 149
Freud, S. xiv–xvi, 1–2, 4, 11, 14, 18, 20, 34–35, 38, 56, 58, 85–86, 92, 104–105, 119, 121–122, 126, 128–129, 133–135, 140, 142, 146, 148, 157, 165, 170, 181
Friar Laurence 73, 76, 78, 80
"full of words" (IV.iv.126) 48

Garden of Eden 7
Gertrude 35, 37, 39–44, 128
Gielgud, Sir John 53
Globe Theatre 83
Green, A. 112

Hamlet xvi, 8, 27, 34–35, 40, 83, 112, 129, 161
Hamlet xiv–xv, 10–11, 18, 35–44, 48, 67, 79, 93, 108, 122, 128, 131, 134
Hazlitt, W. 18, 53
Hecatommithi 3
Heimann, P. 12
Hildebrand, P. 158
Historia Regum Britanniae, The 163
Holinshed, R. 163, 174
Holinshed's Chronicles of England, Scotland and Ireland 163
Honigmann, E. A. J. 3

id 35
"Ides of March are come, The" (III.i.1) 100
Irving, Sir Henry 53
Issacs, S. 12

Jacobean drama 51
Jacobus, M. 87
Johnson, S. 18, 115
Jonson, B. 156
Joyce, James 18
Juliet 7, 66–82, 98
    metaphor of 79
Julius Caesar 84, 92, 107, 112, 137

Keats, John 182
kernel of truth 122
King, H. 20
King John 26
King Lear 2, 9, 25–26, 33, 120, 146, 161, 173, 177
King of Milan 145
King of Naples 158
King of Tunis 146
King Polixenes of Bohemia 19
King, Philip 26
Klein, M. 12, 181
Kohut, H. 4, 87–88, 134–135, 159, 172, 181

Lady Capulet 77, 81
Lady Macbeth 20–25, 42, 134, 147
LaMar, V. A. 165, 171
Laurence Olivier, Sir 53
Lavinia 117, 119, 121, 123–128, 131–132
Lives of Noble Grecians and Romans 84
Loewald, H. W. 157, 178
Lord Capulet 66, 78
loss of energy 164
"lost little girl, the" 19
love,
    and narcissism 158
    and Richard III, 29–30, 34
    Antonio's for Bassanio 55, 61, 64–65
    Antony and Brutus 103, 106
    Antony and Caesar 103
    Brutus and Caesar 105–106, 109–110, 113
    Brutus and Portia 98, 113
    Cassius and Brutus 86, 88–89, 91, 107–108
    Ferdinand and Miranda 146, 149, 151
    Hamlet's for Gertrude 42
    Iago's for Desdemona, removal of 3
    Iago's view of 6–7
    is blind 60
    language of 105
    Macbeth's for the King 22–23
    Mercutio and 69
    objects 56, 82, 153, 172
    Othello and Desdemona 5–6, 11
    Romeo and Juliet 71–73, 75, 81–82
    Romeo and Rosaline 67–68, 73, 75
    test by King Lear 162–163, 165–171, 179
Love's Labour's Lost 26
Lucius 95–96, 108, 117, 121, 127, 131–133

Macbeth 11, 18, 20–25, 122, 134, 147
Macbeth 12, 20, 25, 70, 83, 161
Macduff 24–25
Magic Flute, The 124
Mahler, M. 81
Mark Antony *see* Antony
Martius, Caius 45–46
Measure for Measure 26
melancholy/melancholic 56
    Antonio's 53, 59
    Elizabethan view of 110
    guilt 20
    humours 133
    Portia's 56–57
    Romeo's 67

Merchant of Venice, The 25, 52, 65, 80, 165
Mercutio 69–70, 72–74, 80
Merry Wives of Windsor, The 17
Midsummer Night's Dream, A 8, 26, 56, 115, 156
Miranda 25–26, 138–143, 145–146, 149–150, 152–154, 157–159
mirror transference 87–88
Monmouth, G. 163
moon-calf 144, 149
Moses and Monotheism 92, 170
mother(s)
    absent 25–26
    and absent children 20–25
    and character formation 124
    and Oedipus complex 92
    in *Coriolanus* 44–48
    in *Hamlet* 34–44
    in *Julius Caesar* 111
    in *King Lear* 178
    in *Richard III* 28–34
    in *The Tempest* 140, 144
    in *Titus Andronicus* 118–120
    magical 18–20
    of dead children 26–27
    paucity of 17–18
    present 27–34
Much Ado About Nothing 26
"Mourning and melancholia" 56, 104
"My contact with Josef Popper-Lynkeus" 133

Nemean lion 35

oedipal
    fantasy 19
    issues 174
    objects 20, 157
    phase 35
    situation 44, 82
        female 80

tragedy 112
victory 59
Oedipus xiv, 34, 112–113, 134
    complex 92, 112, 121
Oedipus Rex 34
"On First Looking into Chapman's Homer" 182
Oracle of Delphi, The 19
Othello 3–13, 15, 46, 122, 162
Othello 3, 28, 161

Palmer, D. J. 118
Platter, T. 83
Plutarch 84, 90, 100–101
Pluto's realm 129
Portia (*Merchant of Venice*) 7, 25, 55–60, 62–65, 68, 80–81
Portia (*Julius Caesar*) 98, 100, 108, 113
practical joker, the 13
Prospero 8, 25–26, 138–159
    proto- 73
psychobiography 18, 156

Queen Anne 29
Queen Elizabeth 31, 48, 121
Queen Gertrude 39–40
Queen Mab 69
Queen Margaret 28, 30, 31
Queen of Carthage 147

Redgrave, Sir Michael 53
Richard III 1–3, 27–34, 46, 48, 174
Riviere, J. 12
Roman Empire 117
Romeo, 66–82, 98
Romeo and Juliet 52, 65, 80–81
Rosen, I. 116
Rothenberg, A. 17
Rowe, Nicholas 53
Rustin, Margaret and Michael 23

INDEX

Schiller, Friedrich 27
Shakespeare, William,
   and dead son xv
   and ghosts 109
   and humours 133–134
   and madness 134, 150
   and Merchant of Venice 52–53
   and mothers 17–18, 42
   and nature 56
   and origins of villainy 46
   and women 92, 125
   as actor 156
   characters 1–3, 48, 52
   comedies 60
   death of father xv
   tragedies 51–52, 82, 83, 122, 134
   use of sources 3, 25, 40, 54, 84–85, 100, 163–164
Shaw, George Bernard 14
Sir Thomas 84
Spanish Tragedy, The 35, 118, 121
Spenser, E. 163–164
Steiner, G. 28
Stern, T. 164
superego 35
Sydney, P. 163

"take my milk for gall" (I.v.48) 22
Taming of the Shrew, The 26, 115
Tamora 117–119, 123–126, 131–132
Tempest, The 9, 25, 137, 152, 156, 158–159

Terman, D. 112
Thane of Cawdor 21
"Till then, think of the world" (I.ii.306) 93
Titus 2, 116–124, 126–132, 134–135
Titus Andronicus 115–116, 130, 158
Tobin, A. 173
Tobin, S. 164
Tower of London 26, 29
tragedy 51, 82
Tragedy of King Richard III, The 26, 33, 37, 44, 161
tripartite model 35
True Chronicle History of King Leir, The 164
Two Gentleman of Verona, The 26

Vaughan, A. T. 137
Vaughan, V. M. 137
Venetian lands 6
Verona 66, 70, 75, 80
villains/villainy 1–3, 29, 32, 34, 36, 61, 74–75, 103, 132, 170, 174
Volumnia 22, 44–48

Williams, C. 83
Winnicott, D. W. xiv, 7, 9, 73, 87, 138, 159, 181
Winter's Tale, The 18–20
Wright, L. B. 165, 171